Contents

 KU-541-789

Acknowledgements

We owe a huge debt of thanks to many people, but to four in particular, without whose help this guide could not have been compiled. We have relied heavily on the expertise and detailed book knowledge of Sue Adler and Pam Dix of Islington Education Library Service, who compiled the 12-14 section; and that of Theresa Gibb and Ruth Barnet of Hertfordshire Library Service who made major contributions to the 5-7 and 8-11 sections.

The ideas and imagination of the many people who have contributed have helped to provide a broader scope, and we would like to thank the following:

Sandra Stokes, Sheila Morrow, Kathy Dunsheath, Mark Louden, Valerie Christie and Marie Sloane at the South Eastern Education and Library Board, Northern Ireland;

Hertfordshire Library Service;

Angela McNally, East Sussex Schools Library Service;

Hampshire Library Service;

Jayne Truran and her colleagues in the St Albans Children's Book Group;

Julie Mills at the Learning Resources Centre, Roehampton Institute;

Moira Arthur at Peters Library Services, Birmingham;

Young Book Trust, London

We are grateful to Orchard Books, Oxford University Press and Transworld Publishers for permission to incorporate reproductions of their jacket designs on the cover.

We appreciated the encouragement, particularly in the early stages of the project, of Catherine Davis, Julia Marriage and Anthony Tilke.

We are grateful to our publisher David Spiller, Director of LISU, for his help and support, and also to his colleagues Mary Ashworth and Sharon Fletcher, for their unfailing patience and help in providing a telephone hotline for any problems we encountered, for designing the layout, and for developing the database used in organising the content, with the technical expertise of Goff Sargent.

Finally, one of the best resources of all was the combined expertise of our families - Rebecca Green, Brian and Simon Irvin, Tony, Naomi, Ben and Anna Cooper.

Who Next...?

a guide to children's authors

Edited by Norah Irvin & Lesley Cooper

IRVIN, Norah and COOPER, Lesley, Editors
Who next...? a guide to children's authors

1999

ISBN 1 901786 17 X

© British Library Board 1999

Cover design by
Kathryn Knapman, Audio Visual Services, Loughborough University
using reproductions from original cover images as follows:

City limits: The scam by Bernard Ashley
Double image by Pat Moon
How to eat fried worms by Thomas Rockwell
Humming whispers by Angela Johnson
Love is forever by Jean Ure
Polly the most poetic person by Laurence Anholt, Illus. Tony Ross
Sea of peril by Elizabeth Hawkins
The flight of the ebony owl by Jennifer Carswell Hynd
Tiny Tim by Rose Impey, Illus. Shoo Rayner
Welcome home, Barney by Rose Impey, Illus. Shoo Rayner
courtesy of Orchard Books

A little lower than angels by Geraldine McCaughrean (first published 1987)
Tom's midnight garden by Philippa Pearce (first published 1958)
by permission of Oxford University Press

Pig-heart boy by Malorie Blackman, cover illustration © Derek Brazell
A mouse called wolf by Dick King-Smith
Clockwork or all wound up by Philip Pullman
The creature in the dark by Robert Westall
The Frankenstein teacher by Tony Bradman
The Lottie project by Jacqueline Wilson
The Welkin Weasels: Thunder Oak by Garry Kilworth
by arrangement with Transworld Publishers Ltd.

Printed by
W & G Baird Ltd, Greystone Press, Antrim, N Ireland BT41 2RS

Published and distributed by
The Library and Information Statistics Unit (LISU)
Department of Information Science
Loughborough University, Loughborough, LE11 3TU
Tel: +44 (0)1509 223071 Fax: +44 (0)1509 223072 E-mail: lisu@lboro.ac.uk
http://www.lboro.ac.uk/departments/dils/lisu/lisuhp.html

Introduction

Who next? A guide to children's authors is designed as a tool to help parents, teachers and librarians in schools and public libraries to guide children who have already enjoyed stories by one writer to find other authors they will enjoy reading.

The book lists 400 writers of children's fiction, and with each name suggests other authors who write in a similar way. The idea is that you look up one of your favourite children's authors, then try reading a book by one of the other authors listed underneath. By moving from one entry to another readers can expand the number of writers they enjoy. The same system has been used successfully in a similar guide to adult fiction. Also published by LISU, *Who else writes like? A readers' guide to fiction authors* is now in its third edition.

The links we have made between authors are of genre and theme, and also of styles of writing, or similar aspects of characterisation and settings. Of course no author writes exactly like another, and readers will not agree with all our choices. Questioning *Who next?* may be one of the pleasures of using it, and a source for discussion and debate.

Most of the authors listed have written several books. We have tried to include books that are easily available, so the titles recommended should be obtainable either from a library or from a bookshop. Whilst we recognise their importance in encouraging the love of reading, we decided to exclude picture books, for both younger and older children, as our aim in this book is to focus on story rather than illustration. We have not included books written primarily for adults.

Who next? is arranged by three 'audience age groups': children aged 5-7, 8-11 and 12-14. Where an author writes for more than one age group, this is shown. We have not attempted to define age ranges exactly as this is limiting, and our aim is to encourage children to read as widely as possible. We ask users of *Who next?* to bear in mind the preferences, abilities and needs of individual children.

We have also included in the text a few of the most important titles for each author, so that readers trying an author new to them have some idea of where to start.

At the end of *Who next?* are indexes of authors by theme or genre and children's series, and a list of authors who have won prizes for their children's fiction.

We very much hope that the book will help many readers to enjoy more children's books. Being published for the first time during the National Year of Reading, we also hope it will strike a particularly timely and useful chord. Our intention is to produce a further edition in three years time, so if there are any names you think should be included (or you disagree strongly with any of the recommendations made), please do let us know, through our publisher.

Norah Irvin   *Lesley Cooper*
Stevenage   St Albans

How to use this guide

Author lists

We have arranged the lists of authors by age range then alphabetically by author surname.

So, to use *Who Next*, first select the appropriate age range, 5–7, 8–11 or 12–14. Then, in the alphabetical list, locate the author you want to match. There you find the suggested alternative authors.

For example, a reader who is 10 years old and who likes Jacqueline Wilson books might also enjoy stories by Anne Fine, Hilary McKay or Jean Ure.

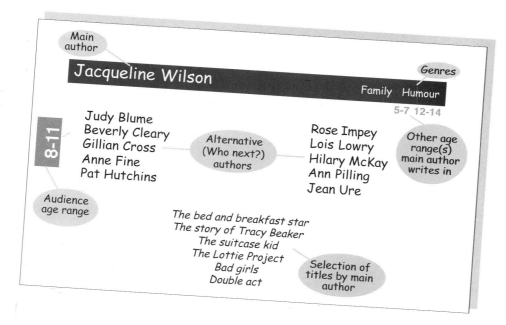

Where an author writes in a theme or genre, this is indicated. Do remember that some authors who frequently write in a particular category or for a specific age group sometimes produce a book in a quite different genre or for another age group. You can check this by reading the jacket details and summaries on the books themselves.

Genres and themes

If you only want a list of authors who write in a particular category or genre, such as Adventure or Animals, then turn straight to the Genre lists which start on page 130.

Series

We have included a list of children's series starting on page 145. Many children's books are published within series and this is often a helpful guide to finding similar authors.

Current children's book prizes for fiction

Stories which have been awarded a special prize are listed on pages 150-158.

How to use this guide

Prizes

The Carnegie Medal

Announced in July

The Carnegie medal is given for an outstanding work of fiction or non-fiction for children. Contenders are appraised for characterisation, plot, style, accuracy, imaginative quality and that indefinable element that lifts a book above the others. (NB The date of this award is based on the year in which the books were published, not in which the award is announced, e.g. the 1993 award was announced in June 1994). Instituted in 1936.

1993	Stone cold	Robert Swindells	Hamish Hamilton
1994	Whispers in the graveyard	Theresa Breslin	Methuen
1995	His dark materials: Northern lights	Philip Pullman	Scholastic
1996	Junk	Melvin Burgess	Andersen Press
1997	River boy	Tim Bowler	Oxford University Press

The Kate Greenaway Medal

Announced in June

The Kate Greenaway Medal goes to an artist who has produced the most distinguished work in the illustration of children's books. The nominated books are assessed for design, format and production as well as artistic merit. The books must be published in the United Kingdom during the preceding year. Instituted in 1955.

1993	Black ships before Troy	Alan Lee	Frances Lincoln
1994	Way home	Gregory Rogers	Andersen Press
1995	The Christmas miracle of Jonathan Toomey	P J Lynch	Walker Books
1996	The baby who wouldn't go to bed	Helen Cooper	Doubleday
1997	When Jessie came across the sea	Amy Hest Illus. P J Lynch	Walker Books

We believe you will find this guide easy to use but please remember, it is not infallible. Finally, if you do need more information, ask. Library and bookshop staff are very willing to help.

Allan Ahlberg
Humour

8-11

Nick Butterworth
Bennett Cerf
John Cunliffe
P J Eastman
Florence Parry Heide

Syd Hoff
Anita Jeram
Theo Le Sieg
Dr Seuss
Pat Thomson

Dinosaur dreams
Mrs Wobble, the waitress
The black cat

Joan Aiken
Fantasy   Historical

8-11 12-14

Eleanor Allen
Leon Garfield

Michael Morpurgo
Jill Paton Walsh

The midnight moropus
The shoemaker's boy
Necklace of raindrops

Eleanor Allen
Ghost/supernatural

Joan Aiken
Jon Blake

Catherine Sefton

Ghost dog
Ghost from the sea
Ghost horse

Jonathan Allen
Humour   Magic

Laurence Anholt
Margaret Stuart Barry

Terence Blacker
Helen Muir

B.I.G. trouble
Potion commotion
The witch who couldn't spell

1

Joy Allen
Family   Humour

Dick Cate
Michael Coleman
Terrance Dicks
Carolyn Dinan
Anne Fine

John Gatehouse
Michael Hardcastle
Thelma Lambert
Ann Pilling

Percy goes on holiday
Percy goes to Spain
Computer for Charlie

Judy Allen
Humour   Animals

12-14

Dick Cate
Jane Gardam
Mary Hooper
Dick King-Smith

Joan Lingard
Margaret Ryan
Dyan Sheldon

Dim thin ducks
The great pig sprint
The most brilliant trick ever

Linda Allen
Humour   Magic

Gyles Brandreth
Angela Bull
Philippa Gregory
Sheila Lavelle

Kara May
Catherine Sefton
Kaye Umansky

Mrs Simkin and the wishing well
Mrs Simkin and the magic wheelbarrow
Mrs Simkin and the groovy old gramophone

Heather Amery
Animals   Humour

Alan Baron   Gillian Osband

The grumpy goat
The hungry donkey
Pig gets stuck

Rachel Anderson
Family

12-14

Angela Bull   Penelope Lively
Shirley Hughes   Ann Pilling
Rose Impey

Jessy runs away
Jessy and the bridesmaid's dress
Best friends

Scoular Anderson
Adventure   Humour

Felicity Everett   Margaret Joy
Rose Impey   Pat Thomson
Julia Jarman

Amazing Mark in Creepstone Castle
Changing Charlie
Clogpots in space

Laurence Anholt
Humour

Jonathan Allen   Terry Deary
Jon Blake   Robert Leeson
Keith Brumpton   Marjorie Newman
Roald Dahl   Bob Wilson

Polly the most poetic person
Daft Jack and the beanstack
Rumply Crumply Stinky Pin

Phyllis Arkle — Animals

Henrietta Branford
Stan Cullimore
Dick King-Smith

Tessa Krailing
Jill Tomlinson
Colin West

The railway cat and the ghost
The railway cat on the run
The railway cat's secret

Brian Ball — Animals Family Humour School

Harriet Castor
Michael Coleman
June Crebbin
Carolyn Dinan
Adèle Geras

Rose Impey
Dick King-Smith
Thelma Lambert
Hilda Offen
Rosemary Sutcliff

Bella's concert
Bella and the beanstalk
Bella at the ballet

Jill Barklem — Animals

Beatrix Potter
Jill Tomlinson

Alison Uttley

Brambly Hedge

Alan Baron — Animals Humour

Heather Amery
Rose Impey
Anita Jeram

Tony Kerins
Colin West

Red Fox and the baby bunnies
Red Fox dances
Red Fox monster

Margaret Stuart Barry Fantasy Humour Magic

5-7

Jonathan Allen
Terence Blacker
June Crebbin

Sheila Lavelle
Penelope Lively
Helen Muir

Diz and the big fat burglar
Simon and the witch
Simon and the witch in school

S and J Berenstain Humour

P J Eastman
Syd Hoff
Anita Jeram

Theo Le Sieg
Dr Seuss
Colin West

Berenstain bears on the moon
Berenstain bears in the night
Berenstain bears on wheels

Terence Blacker Fantasy Humour Magic

8-11

Jonathan Allen
Margaret Stuart Barry

Helen Muir

In control, Ms Wiz?
Ms Wiz banned
Ms Wiz supermodel

Malorie Blackman Adventure

8-11 12-14

Ruskin Bond
Lisa Bruce
Ann Cameron

Jamila Gavin
Julia Jarman
Errol Lloyd

Betsy Biggelow: Hurricane Betsy
Betsy Biggelow is here!
Betsy Biggelow the detective

Jon Blake   Adventure Ghost/supernatural Humour Science fiction

Eleanor Allen
Laurence Anholt
Gyles Brandreth

Douglas Hill
Michael Lawrence

F.S. 3
Ghost of Joseph Grey

Michael Bond   Humour

8-11

Vivian French   Shoo Rayner

Paddington breaks the peace
Paddington's disappearing trick
Paddington's picnic

Ruskin Bond   Family

Malorie Blackman
Lisa Bruce

Ann Cameron
Jamila Gavin

Snake trouble
Cricket for the crocodile
Getting Granny's glasses

Tony Bradman   Animals Fantasy Humour

8-11

Damon Burnard
Stan Cullimore
Terrance Dicks
Anne Forsyth
Vivian French

Douglas Hill
Tessa Krailing
Margaret Nash
John Ryan
Ross Thomson

Dilly the dinosaur
Search for the Saucy Sally
Revenge at Ryan's Reef

Franz Brandenberg
Family   Humour

5-7

Rob Lewis   Jean Van Leeuwen
James Marshall

Leo and Emily
Leo and Emily's big ideas

Gyles Brandreth
Adventure   Humour   Magic

8-11

Linda Allen   Brough Girling
Jon Blake   Philippa Gregory
Jeff Brown   Ann Jungman
Terrance Dicks   Sheila Lavelle
Andrew Donkin   Wes Magee

The slippers that talked
The slippers that answered back
The slippers that sneezed

Henrietta Branford
Animals   Humour

8-11 12-14

Phyllis Arkle   Jill Tomlinson

Royal Blunder
Royal Blunder and the haunted house

Jeff Brown
Adventure   Fantasy   Humour

Gyles Brandreth   Florence Parry Heide
Patrick Skene Catling   Sam McBratney
Terry Deary   Alexander McCall-Smith
Anne Fine   Alf Proysen

Flat Stanley
Invisible Stanley
Stanley in space

Lisa Bruce Adventure

Malorie Blackman
Ruskin Bond
Ann Cameron
Michael Coleman
Jamila Gavin

Geraldine McCaughrean
Kara May
Hilda Offen
Karen Wallace

Dynamite Deela: Double trouble
Dynamite Deela: Muddle trouble
Jazeera in the sun

Keith Brumpton Humour

Laurence Anholt
Damon Burnard
Stan Cullimore
Roald Dahl

Terry Deary
Sam McBratney
Martin Waddell

Four legged sheriff
Look out Loch Ness Monster
Tanya hoofed crusader

Angela Bull Family

8-11

Linda Allen
Rachel Anderson
Terrance Dicks
John Escott

Jane Gardam
Michael Hardcastle
Ann Pilling

Green gloves
Pink socks
Yellow wellies

Janet Burchett and Sarah Vogler Humour   Sport

Rob Childs
Michael Coleman

Michael Hardcastle
Martin Waddell

The Tigers: The cup final
The Tigers: Save the pitch
The Tigers: The terrible trainer

Damon Burnard   Animals

Tony Bradman

Keith Brumpton

Bullysaurus

Nick Butterworth   Humour

Allan Ahlberg

John Cunliffe

After the storm
The rescue party
The fox's hiccups

Ann Cameron   Family

Malorie Blackman
Ruskin Bond
Lisa Bruce
Jamila Gavin

Julia Jarman
Errol Lloyd
Alexander McCall-Smith

The Julian stories
Julian, dream doctor
Julian, secret agent

Harriet Castor
Animals Humour

8-11

Brian Ball
Vivian French
Margaret Gordon

Ivan Jones
Penelope Lively
Shoo Rayner

Fat Puss and friends
Fat Puss and Slimpup
Fat Puss on wheels

Dick Cate
Family Humour

Joy Allen
Judy Allen

Thelma Lambert

Ben's big day
Bernard's magic
Bernard's prize

Patrick Skene Catling
Fantasy Humour Magic

Jeff Brown
Anne Fine

Sam McBratney
Alexander McCall-Smith

The chocolate touch II
John Midas and the radio touch

Kathryn Cave
Animals Fantasy Humour

Anne Forsyth

Ann Ruffell

Dragonrise
Jumble
The emperor's gruckle hound

Bennett Cerf

Allan Ahlberg
P J Eastman

Dr Seuss

Book of animal riddles
Book of riddles
More riddles

Rob Childs

Sport

8-11

Janet Burchett and
Sarah Vogler

Michael Coleman
Michael Hardcastle

The big break
The big chance
The big game

Michael Coleman

Humour   School   Sport

8-11

Joy Allen
Brian Ball
Lisa Bruce
Janet Burchett and
   Sarah Vogler
Rob Childs

Mary Hooper
Geraldine McCaughrean
Wes Magee
Hiawyn Oram
Karen Wallace

Fizzy hits the headlines
Fizzy steals the show
Fizzy TV star

June Crebbin

Humour

Brian Ball
Margaret Stuart Barry

Penelope Lively

Fly by night
Ride to the rescue
The curse of the skull

Helen Cresswell
Fantasy   Humour

8-11

Brough Girling
Philippa Gregory
Margaret Joy
Ann Jungman

Ann Ruffell
Margaret Ryan
Pat Thomson

Almost goodbye Guzzler
Dragon ride
Two hoots

Stan Cullimore
Animals   Family   Humour

Phyllis Arkle
Tony Bradman
Keith Brumpton

Terrance Dicks
Dorothy Edwards
Jill Tomlinson

Henrietta and the magic trick
Henrietta's night out
Henrietta's pocket money

John Cunliffe
Humour

Allan Ahlberg

Nick Butterworth

Postman Pat gets fat
Postman Pat plant sitter
Postman Pat's white Christmas

Roald Dahl
Humour

8-11

Laurence Anholt
Keith Brumpton
Terry Deary

Sam McBratney
Bob Wilson

Fantastic Mr Fox
The Twits
Magic finger

Terry Deary

Laurence Anholt
Jeff Brown
Keith Brumpton

Roald Dahl
Sam McBratney

Joke factory
Magic of the museum
The treasure of Crazy Horse

Terrance Dicks

Adventure   Animals   Family   Humour

8-11

Joy Allen
Tony Bradman
Gyles Brandreth
Angela Bull
Stan Cullimore

John Escott
Anne Forsyth
Brough Girling
Michael Hardcastle
Ann Pilling

George and the dragon
Lost property
T.R. Bear

Carolyn Dinan

Family

Joy Allen
Brian Ball
John Gatehouse

Thelma Lambert
Joan Lingard
Catherine Sefton

A dog would be better
Goodnight monster
The witch's birthday present

Andrew Donkin

Adventure   Ghost/supernatural

Gyles Brandreth
Sarah Garland

Sam McBratney

The bugman
Night skies
Colour me crazy

13

P J Eastman

Animals   Humour

Allan Ahlberg
S and J Berenstain
Bennett Cerf

Sarah Hayes
Dr Seuss

Are you my mother?
Go dog go
Sam and the firefly

Dorothy Edwards

Family   Humour

Stan Cullimore
Mary Hoffman

Shirley Hughes
Alf Proysen

My naughty little sister

John Escott

Family

Angela Bull
Terrance Dicks

Michael Hardcastle
Ann Pilling

Matthew's surprise
Wayne's luck
Wayne's wedding

Felicity Everett

Adventure

Scoular Anderson
Brough Girling

Kara May

Saturday Spies in a twist in the tale
Saturday Spies in the cat's pyjamas

Anne Fine

Fantasy   Magic

8-11 12-14

Joy Allen
Jeff Brown
Patrick Skene Catling
Anne Forsyth
Jane Gardam

Adèle Geras
Thelma Lambert
Robert Leeson
Wes Magee
Jan Mark

A sudden glow of gold
A sudden puff of glittering smoke
A sudden gust of icy wind

Anne Forsyth

Adventure   Animals   Family   Fantasy

Tony Bradman
Kathryn Cave
Terrance Dicks
Anne Fine

Adèle Geras
Wes Magee
Jan Mark
Ann Ruffell

Mostly magic
Library monster
Wedding day scramble

Vivian French

Animals   Humour

Michael Bond
Tony Bradman
Harriet Castor
Ivan Jones
Arnold Lobel

Gillian Osband
Shoo Rayner
Angie Sage
Pat Thomson
Martin Waddell

Hedgehogs and the big bag
Hedgehogs don't eat hamburgers
Morris and the catflap

Jane Gardam

Animals Environment Family

Judy Allen
Angela Bull
Anne Fine

Dick King-Smith
Jan Mark

Tufty bear
Black woolly pony
Bridget and William

Leon Garfield

Historical

8-11 12-14

Joan Aiken
Michael Morpurgo

Jill Paton Walsh

Fair's fair
The sabre-tooth sandwich

Sarah Garland

Adventure

Andrew Donkin
Brough Girling

Robin Kingsland
Sam McBratney

Clive and the missing finger
Dad on the run
Madame Sizzers

John Gatehouse

Animals Humour

Joy Allen
Carolyn Dinan

Ivan Jones
Colin West

Eric's elephant
Eric's elephant on holiday
Eric's elephant goes camping

Susan Gates

Animals   School

Jana Novotny Hunter
Dick King-Smith
Tessa Krailing

Wes Magee
Margaret Nash
Rosemary Sutcliff

Esther and the baby baboon
Pet swapping day
Whizz bang and the crocodile room

Jamila Gavin

Family   Friends

8-11 12-14

Malorie Blackman
Ruskin Bond

Lisa Bruce
Ann Cameron

Kamla and Kate
Kamla and Kate again
Deadly friends

Adèle Geras

Animals   Family

8-11 12-14

Brian Ball
Anne Fine
Anne Forsyth
Dick King-Smith

Jan Mark
Pat Moon
Ann Ruffell

Fish pie for flamingoes
The glittering river
The strange bird

Brough Girling

Adventure   Humour

8-11

Gyles Brandreth
Helen Cresswell
Terrance Dicks
Felicity Everett
Sarah Garland

Robin Kingsland
Frank Rodgers
Dyan Sheldon
Pat Thomson

Clever Trevor
Nora Bone
Nora Bone and the Tooth Fairy

17

Margaret Gordon · Animals

Harriet Castor
Ivan Jones

Dick King-Smith

Help!
Willie Whiskers

Mick Gowar · Adventure Historical Humour

Mary Hooper
Robin Kingsland

Michael Lawrence
Karen Wallace

The great necklace hunt
The guard dog geese
The lost legionary

Philippa Gregory · Magic

Linda Allen
Gyles Brandreth
Helen Cresswell

Ann Jungman
Ann Ruffell

Diggory the Boa Conductor
The little pet dragon

Michael Hardcastle · Family

8-11

Joy Allen
Angela Bull
Janet Burchett and
   Sarah Vogler

Rob Childs
Terrance Dicks
John Escott
Ann Pilling

James and the TV star
Joanna's goal
The magic party

Colin and Jacqui Hawkins Humour

5-7

Sarah Hayes
Hiawyn Oram
Gerald Rose

Dr Seuss
Kaye Umansky

Pirates
Spooks

Sarah Hayes Humour

P J Eastman
Colin and Jacqui Hawkins
Gerald Rose

Dr Seuss
Colin West

This is the bear
This is the bear and the picnic lunch

Florence Parry Heide Fantasy

Allan Ahlberg
Jeff Brown

Sheila Lavelle
Alf Proysen

The shrinking of Treehorn
Treehorn's treasure

Douglas Hill Fantasy

8-11

Jon Blake
Tony Bradman
Julia Jarman

Penelope Lively
Frank Rodgers

The moon monsters
The unicorn dream
How Jennifer (and Speckle) saved the world

Syd Hoff
Humour

Allan Ahlberg
S and J Berenstain

Pat Thomson

Bernard on his own
Danny and the dinosaur
Stanley

Mary Hoffman
Adventure   Fantasy   Humour

Dorothy Edwards
Sheila Lavelle

Catherine Sefton

Max in the jungle
Min's first jump
King of the castle

Mary Hooper
Family   Historical   Humour

8-11 12-14

Judy Allen
Michael Coleman
Mick Gowar

Michael Lawrence
Karen Wallace
Jacqueline Wilson

The golden key
The ghoul at school
Round the rainbow

Shirley Hughes
Family   Humour

Rachel Anderson

Dorothy Edwards

Chips and Jessie
It's too frightening for me
Charlie Moon

Jana Novotny Hunter

Susan Gates
Ann Jungman
Tessa Krailing

Frank Rodgers
Hazel Townson

Hector's ghost
Hector the spectre
Pet detectives: Polly and Rick's casebook

Rose Impey

Animals Family Humour

8-11

Rachel Anderson
Scoular Anderson
Brian Ball
Alan Baron
Margaret Joy

Pat Moon
Michael Morpurgo
Hiawyn Oram
Gillian Osband
Colin West

Tiny Tim the longest jumping frog
Welcome home Barney
Houdini dog

Julia Jarman

Adventure

8-11

Scoular Anderson
Malorie Blackman
Ann Cameron
Douglas Hill

Robin Kingsland
Michael Lawrence
Chris Powling
Pat Thomson

Georgie and the dragon
Georgie and the computer bugs
Georgie and the planet raider

Anita Jeram
Animals   Humour

Allan Ahlberg
Alan Baron
S and J Berenstain

Tony Kerins
Colin West

Birthday happy, Contrary Mary
Contrary Mary
Daisy Dare

Ivan Jones
Animals   Humour

Harriet Castor
Vivian French
John Gatehouse

Margaret Gordon
Shoo Rayner

Zot goes camping
Zot solves it
Zot's treasure

Margaret Joy
Adventure   School

Scoular Anderson
Helen Cresswell
Rose Impey
Ann Jungman

Robert Leeson
Wes Magee
Margaret Nash
Jean Ure

Tales of the Allotment Lane School
Fifi and Slug
The little explorer

Ann Jungman
Adventure   Humour   Magic

8-11

Gyles Brandreth
Helen Cresswell
Philippa Gregory

Jana Novotny Hunter
Margaret Joy

Leila's magical monster party
Little Luis and the bad bandit
There's a troll at the bottom of my garden

Tony Kerins

Animals Humour

5-7

Alan Baron
Anita Jeram

Colin West

The brave ones
Little Clancy's new drum

Dick King-Smith

Animals Humour

8-11

Judy Allen
Phyllis Arkle
Brian Ball
Jane Gardam
Susan Gates

Adèle Geras
Margaret Gordon
Tessa Krailing
Hiawyn Oram
Rosemary Sutcliff

Blessu
Dumpling
Happy Mouseday

Robin Kingsland

Adventure Humour

Sarah Garland
Brough Girling
Mick Gowar
Julia Jarman
Joan Lingard

Sam McBratney
Chris Powling
Gerald Rose
Pat Thomson
Jacqueline Wilson

Mo and the mummy case
Cowardly cutlass
Doghouse Reilly

Tessa Krailing
Animals

8-11

Phyllis Arkle
Tony Bradman
Susan Gates

Jana Novotny Hunter
Dick King-Smith

The cat burglar
The donkey rescue
Trixie and the cyber pet

Thelma Lambert
Family   Humour

Joy Allen
Brian Ball
Dick Cate
Carolyn Dinan
Anne Fine

Sheila Lavelle
Joan Lingard
Jan Mark
Ann Pilling
Catherine Sefton

Messy Maisy
Benny's night out
The half term rabbit

Sheila Lavelle
Humour   Magic

8-11

Linda Allen
Margaret Stuart Barry
Gyles Brandreth
Florence Parry Heide

Mary Hoffman
Thelma Lambert
Catherine Sefton
Kaye Umansky

Ursula Series
Harry's dog
Harry's cat

Michael Lawrence
Historical

Jon Blake
Mick Gowar
Mary Hooper

Julia Jarman
Karen Wallace

Mystery at the Globe

Theo Le Sieg — Humour

Allan Ahlberg
S and J Berenstain

Dr Seuss

Hooper Humperdink? Not him
In a people house
Please try to remember the first of October

Robert Leeson — Adventure Fantasy Humour School

8-11 12-14

Laurence Anholt
Anne Fine
Margaret Joy
Wes Magee

Margaret Nash
Marjorie Newman
Jean Ure

April fool at Hoblane school
Ghosts at Hoblane school
Pancake pickle

Rob Lewis — Family Humour

Franz Brandenberg
James Marshall

E H Minarik
Jean Van Leeuwen

Grandpa comes to stay
Grandpa on holiday
Too much trouble for Grandpa

Joan Lingard — Family

12-14

Judy Allen
Carolyn Dinan
Robin Kingsland

Thelma Lambert
Gerald Rose

Clever Clive/Loopy Lucy
Secrets and surprises
Sulky Suzy/Jittery Jack

Penelope Lively

8-11 12-14

Rachel Anderson
Margaret Stuart Barry
Harriet Castor

June Crebbin
Douglas Hill
Ann Ruffell

Staying with Grandpa
Two bears and Joe

Errol Lloyd

Family

12-14

Malorie Blackman

Ann Cameron

Sasha and the bicycle thieves
Big gold robbery

Arnold Lobel

Animals   Humour

Vivian French
James Marshall
E H Minarik
Gillian Osband

Shoo Rayner
Jean Van Leeuwen
Max Velthuijs
Martin Waddell

Days with Frog and Toad
Mouse tales
Owl at home

Sam McBratney

Adventure   Humour

Jeff Brown
Keith Brumpton
Patrick Skene Catling
Roald Dahl
Terry Deary

Andrew Donkin
Sarah Garland
Robin Kingsland
Pat Thomson

Francis Fry and the O.T.G.
Francis Fry, Private Eye
Hurrah for Flash Eddie

Alexander McCall-Smith

Jeff Brown
Ann Cameron

Patrick Skene Catling
Frank Rodgers

Akimbo and the Crocodile Man
The banana machine
Calculator Annie

Geraldine McCaughrean

Lisa Bruce
Michael Coleman

Kara May
Hiawyn Oram

Wizziwig and the flying car
Wizziwig and the sweet machine
Wizziwig and the weather machine

Wes Magee

Gyles Brandreth
Michael Coleman
Anne Fine
Anne Forsyth
Susan Gates

Margaret Joy
Robert Leeson
Margaret Nash
Hazel Townson

The Scumbagg School scorpion
The spookspotters of Scumbagg School
Sports Day at Scumbagg School

Jan Mark

Anne Fine
Anne Forsyth
Jane Gardam

Adèle Geras
Thelma Lambert

The twig thing
Snow maze

James Marshall Animals   Humour

Franz Brandenberg
Rob Lewis
Arnold Lobel
E H Minarik

Shoo Rayner
Jean Van Leeuwen
Max Velthuijs

Fox and his friends
Fox at school
Fox on wheels

Kara May Adventure   Humour

Linda Allen
Lisa Bruce
Felicity Everett

Geraldine McCaughrean
Hilda Offen
Karen Wallace

Emily H and the enormous tarantula
Emily H and the stranger in the castle
Emily H turns detective

E H Minarik Animals   Humour

Rob Lewis
Arnold Lobel
James Marshall

Jean Van Leeuwen
Max Velthuijs

Father Bear comes home
Little Bear's friends
Little Bear's visit

Pat Moon Animals   Humour

12-14

Adèle Geras
Rose Impey

Michael Morpurgo
Hiawyn Oram

Just you wait Turtle
Ready steady Cheetah
What's up Chimp

Michael Morpurgo

Animals Historical Humour

8-11 12-14

5-7

Joan Aiken
Leon Garfield
Rose Impey
Pat Moon

Hiawyn Oram
Jill Paton Walsh
Colin West

Butterfly lion
Jigger's day off
Red eyes at night

Helen Muir

Fantasy Humour Magic

Jonathan Allen
Margaret Stuart Barry

Terence Blacker

The twenty ton chocolate mountain
Wonderwitch
Wonderwitch and the spooks

Margaret Nash

Humour School

Tony Bradman
Susan Gates
Margaret Joy

Robert Leeson
Wes Magee

Class 1 on the move
Class 1 spells trouble
Enough is enough

Marjorie Newman

Adventure Fantasy Humour

Laurence Anholt
Robert Leeson
John Ryan
Margaret Ryan

Ross Thomson
Kaye Umansky
Colin West

The pirates and Captain Bullseye
The pirates and the spring cleaning
The pirates' big cleanout

Hilda Offen

Brian Ball
Lisa Bruce

Kara May
Hiawyn Oram

Happy Christmas Rita
Rita the rescuer
SOS for Rita

Hiawyn Oram
Animals   Humour

Michael Coleman
Colin and Jacqui Hawkins
Rose Impey
Dick King-Smith

Geraldine McCaughrean
Pat Moon
Michael Morpurgo
Hilda Offen

Cat in a corner
Dog in danger
Dolphin SOS

Gillian Osband
Animals   Humour

Heather Amery
Vivian French
Rose Impey

Arnold Lobel
Shoo Rayner
Martin Waddell

Farmer Jane
Farmer Jane and the birthday treat

Ann Pilling
Family   Humour

8-11

Joy Allen
Rachel Anderson
Angela Bull
Terrance Dicks

John Escott
Michael Hardcastle
Thelma Lambert
Jacqueline Wilson

Bella's dragon
The Friday parcel
The jungle sale

Beatrix Potter

Jill Barklem
Jill Tomlinson

Alison Uttley

The tale of Benjamin Bunny
The tale of Peter Rabbit

Chris Powling

Julia Jarman
Robin Kingsland
Margaret Ryan

Dyan Sheldon
Pat Thomson
Bob Wilson

Harry moves house
Harry's party
Hiccup Harry

Alf Proysen

Jeff Brown
Dorothy Edwards

Florence Parry Heide

Mistress Pepperpot stories
Mrs Pepperpot in the magic wood
Mrs Pepperpot to the rescue

Shoo Rayner

Michael Bond
Harriet Castor
Vivian French
Ivan Jones
Arnold Lobel

James Marshall
Gillian Osband
Angie Sage
Martin Waddell

Charlie's night out
Cyril's cat and the big surprise
Cyril's cat: Mouse practice

Frank Rodgers — Humour

Brough Girling
Douglas Hill
Jana Novotny Hunter

Alexander McCall-Smith
Hazel Townson
Martin Waddell

Bumps in the night
Rattle and Hum, robot detectives
Ricky, Zedex and the spooks

Gerald Rose — Humour

Colin and Jacqui Hawkins
Sarah Hayes

Robin Kingsland
Joan Lingard

Lucy's monster holiday
Tom's dark journey
Penguins in a stew

Ann Ruffell — Fantasy   Humour   Magic

Kathryn Cave
Helen Cresswell
Anne Forsyth

Adèle Geras
Philippa Gregory
Penelope Lively

The pirate band
Dragon water
Mr Wellington Boots - 3 magical stories

John Ryan — Humour

Tony Bradman
Marjorie Newman

Ross Thomson

Admiral Fatso Fitzpugwash
Captain Pugwash and the Pigwig
Sir Cumference and little Daisy

Margaret Ryan — Humour

Judy Allen
Helen Cresswell
Marjorie Newman

Chris Powling
Dyan Sheldon

Charlie and Biff
The littlest dragon
Millie Morgan, pirate

Angie Sage — Animals   Humour

Vivian French
Shoo Rayner

Martin Waddell

The little blue book of the Marie Celeste
The little green book of the last lost dinosaur
The little pink book of the wooly mammoth

Catherine Sefton — Ghost/supernatural   Humour   Magic

8-11

Eleanor Allen
Linda Allen
Carolyn Dinan
Mary Hoffman
Thelma Lambert

Sheila Lavelle
Kaye Umansky
Martin Waddell
Jill Paton Walsh

The Boggart in the barrel
The day the smells went wrong
The ghost ship

Dr Seuss — Humour

Allan Ahlberg
S and J Berenstain
Bennett Cerf
P J Eastman

Colin and Jacqui Hawkins
Sarah Hayes
Theo Le Sieg

Cat in the hat
Green eggs and ham
One fish, two fish, green fish, blue fish

Dyan Sheldon — Humour

Judy Allen
Brough Girling

Chris Powling
Margaret Ryan

Harry and chicken
Harry the explorer
Harry's holiday

Rosemary Sutcliff — Animals

8-11 12-14

Brian Ball
Susan Gates

Dick King-Smith

Little hound found
The roundabout horse

Pat Thomson — Family Humour

Allan Ahlberg
Scoular Anderson
Helen Cresswell
Vivian French
Brough Girling

Syd Hoff
Julia Jarman
Robin Kingsland
Sam McBratney
Chris Powling

Best pest
Thank you for the tadpole
Treasure sock

Ross Thomson — Humour

Tony Bradman
Marjorie Newman

John Ryan

Captain Jones and the ghost ship
Captain Jones's bones

Jill Tomlinson — Animals Humour

Phyllis Arkle
Jill Barklem
Henrietta Branford

Stan Cullimore
Beatrix Potter
Alison Uttley

The owl who was afraid of the dark
The cat who wanted to go home
The hen who wouldn't give up

Hazel Townson — Humour

Jana Novotny Hunter
Wes Magee

Frank Rodgers
Jacqueline Wilson

Blue magic
Amos Shrike, the school ghost
Snakes alive

Kaye Umansky — Fantasy Humour Magic

8-11

Linda Allen
Colin and Jacqui Hawkins
Sheila Lavelle

Marjorie Newman
Catherine Sefton
Jean Ure

The jealous giant
The romantic giant
Sir Quinton Quest hunts the jewel

Jean Ure

8-11 12-14

Margaret Joy
Robert Leeson

Kaye Umansky

Wizard and the witch
Wizard in the woods
Woodside School: Soppy birthday

Alison Uttley

Animals

8-11

Jill Barklem
Beatrix Potter

Jill Tomlinson

How Little Grey Rabbit got back her tail

Jean Van Leeuwen

Animals   Humour

Franz Brandenberg
Rob Lewis
Arnold Lobel

James Marshall
E H Minarik

Oliver Pig at school
More tales of Oliver Pig
Tales of Oliver Pig

Max Velthuijs

Humour

Arnold Lobel
James Marshall

E H Minarik

Frog in winter
Frog is frightened
Frog is a hero

Martin Waddell

Animals   Humour

8-11

5-7

Keith Brumpton
Janet Burchett and
   Sarah Vogler
Vivian French
Arnold Lobel

Gillian Osband
Shoo Rayner
Frank Rodgers
Angie Sage
Catherine Sefton

The get away hen
The lucky duck song

Karen Wallace

Adventure   Humour

Lisa Bruce
Michael Coleman
Mick Gowar

Mary Hooper
Kara May
Michael Lawrence

Flash Harriet and the fiendishly wicked whistle mystery
Flash Harriet and the giant vegetable monster mystery
Flash Harriet and the outrageous ostrich egg mystery

Jill Paton Walsh

Fantasy   Ghost/supernatural   Historical

12-14

Joan Aiken
Leon Garfield

Michael Morpurgo
Catherine Sefton

Thomas and the tinners
Birdy and the ghosties
Matthew and the sea singer

37

Colin West Animals   Humour

Phyllis Arkle
Alan Baron
S and J Berenstain
John Gatehouse
Sarah Hayes

Rose Impey
Anita Jeram
Tony Kerins
Michael Morpurgo
Marjorie Newman

Buzz Buzz went Bumble Bee
I don't care said the Bear
Only joking laughed the Lobster

Bob Wilson Humour

Laurence Anholt
Roald Dahl

Chris Powling

Bing bang boogie, it's a boy scout
Ging gang goolie, it's an alien
Stone the crows, it's a vacuum cleaner

Jacqueline Wilson Adventure   Humour

8-11 12-14

Mary Hooper
Robin Kingsland

Ann Pilling
Hazel Townson

The dinosaur's packed lunch
Cliffhanger
The monster in the cupboard

Authors for ages 8-11

Allan Ahlberg

Family   Fantasy   Humour

5-7

Alan Coren
Jeremy Strong

David Henry Wilson

Woof
Better Brown stories
Giant baby

Joan Aiken

Adventure   Family   Fantasy

5-7 12-14

Clare Bevan
Helen Cresswell
Kevin Crossley-Holland
Diana Wynne Jones

Terry Jones
Garry Kilworth
Philip Pullman

Black hearts in Battersea
Midnight is a place
Mortimer and Arabel
Mortimer and the sword Excalibur

Vivien Alcock

Family   Fantasy   Ghost/supernatural

12-14

Clare Bevan
Angela Bull
Annie Dalton

Rachel Dixon
Jenny Nimmo

Haunting of Cassie Palmer
The cuckoo sister

Louisa May Alcott

Family

Susan M Coolidge
L M Montgomery

Johanna Spyri
Laura Ingalls Wilder

Little women
Good wives
Jo's boys

Roy Apps

Humphrey Carpenter   Paul Jennings
Morris Gleitzman

The genius academy
The haunting
Melvin and the deadheads: Melvin the avenger

Bernard Ashley

12-14

Anne Fine   Jan Mark
Gene Kemp   Jean Ure
Robert Leeson

Roller madonnas
Justin and the demon drop kick
Your guess is as good as mine

Julian Atterton

Kevin Crossley-Holland   Terry Jones
Monica Furlong   Rosemary Sutcliff
Cynthia Harnett   Henry Treece

Knights of the sacred blade
Knights of the lost domain
Robin Hood and Little John

Enid Bagnold

Mary O'Hara   Christine Pullein-Thompson
K M Peyton   Anna Sewell

National Velvet

Lynne Reid Banks

Family Fantasy

12-14

8-11

E Nesbit
Mary Norton

Sylvia Waugh

Indian in the cupboard
Fairy rebel
Return of the Indian
The secret of the Indian

Antonia Barber

Ballet Historical Stage

Harriet Castor
Jean Estoril

Lorna Hill

Dancing shoes: Into the spotlight
Dancing shoes: Lessons for Lucy
The ring in the rough stuff

J M Barrie

Fantasy

Frank L Baum
Lewis Carroll
C S Lewis

P L Travers
Sylvia Waugh

Peter Pan

Frank L Baum

Fantasy

J M Barrie
Lewis Carroll

C S Lewis
P L Travers

The wonderful wizard of Oz
The emerald city of Oz
Dorothy and the wizard in Oz

Nina Bawden Adventure Family War 1939-45

12-14

Berlie Doherty
Judith Kerr

Michelle Magorian
Ann Turnbull

Handful of thieves
Peppermint pig
The finding

Nina Beachcroft Fantasy

Helen Cresswell
Penelope Farmer
Diana Wynne Jones

Penelope Lively
Jenny Nimmo
Philippa Pearce

Well met by witchlight
Under the enchanter
Spell of sleep
Cold Christmas

Elisabeth Beresford Adventure Animals Fantasy

Michael Bond
Dick King-Smith

A A Milne
Mary Norton

Wombles
Wombles at work
Wombles to the rescue
The invisible Womble

Judith M Berrisford Pony/horse

Bonnie Bryant
Joanna Campbell
Wendy Douthwaite

Ruby Ferguson
K M Peyton
Christine Pullein-Thompson

Jackie and the phantom ponies
Jackie on Pony Island

Clare Bevan
Family   Fantasy

Joan Aiken
Vivien Alcock

Angela Bull
Diana Hendry

Roz and Cromarty
Ask me no questions
Mightier than the sword

8-11

Terence Blacker
Computers   Humour   Sport

5-7

Tony Bradman
Humphrey Carpenter
Rob Childs
Michael Coleman

Michael Hardcastle
Bill Naughton
Martin Waddell

Dream team
Shooting star
The transfer

Malorie Blackman
Adventure   Computers

5-7 12-14

Michael Coleman
Gillian Cross
Jamila Gavin

Rosa Guy
Julia Jarman
Ruth Thomas

Gadget man
Thief
A.N.T.I.D.O.T.E.

Judy Blume

12-14

Betsy Byars
Gillian Cross
Paula Danziger
Anne Fine

Robin Klein
Sheila Lavelle
Lois Lowry
Jacqueline Wilson

Blubber
Superfudge
Tales of a fourth grade nothing
Are you there God it's me Margaret
Fudge-a-mania

Enid Blyton

Elinor M Brent-Dyer
Anne Digby
Franklin W Dixon
Allan Frewin Jones
Carolyn Keene

Fiona Kelly
Anthony Masters
Arthur Ransome
Malcolm Saville

Five on a treasure island
Castle of adventure
Good old Secret Seven

Michael Bond

5-7

Elisabeth Beresford

A A Milne

Bear called Paddington
Olga da Polga
Paddington helps out
Paddington abroad

Lucy M Boston

8-11

Adventure   Family   Fantasy

Penelope Farmer
Penelope Lively
E Nesbit
Philippa Pearce

P L Travers
Alison Uttley
Sylvia Waugh

Children of Green Knowe
Chimneys of Green Knowe
River at Green Knowe

Tony Bradman

Adventure Fantasy Humour Sport

5-7

Terence Blacker
Gyles Brandreth
Rob Childs

Terrance Dicks
Jeremy Strong

Sam the girl detective
Frankenstein teacher
Football fever

Gyles Brandreth

Adventure Fantasy Humour

5-7

Tony Bradman
Humphrey Carpenter
Judy Corbalis
Terrance Dicks

Brough Girling
Jill Murphy
Chris Powling

Monsters at no. 13
Ghost at no. 13
Mermaid at no. 13

Henrietta Branford

Adventure Humour

5-7 12-14

Sid Fleischman
Pat Hutchins

Jeremy Strong

Dimanche Diller
Dimanche Diller in danger

Elinor M Brent-Dyer School

8-11

Enid Blyton
Susan M Coolidge

Anne Digby

School at the Chalet
Jo of the Chalet School

Joyce Lancaster Brisley Family Humour

Beverly Cleary
Eve Garnett

Bel Mooney

Milly Molly Mandy

Bonnie Bryant Pony/horse

Judith M Berrisford
Joanna Campbell
Monica Dickens
Wendy Douthwaite

Ruby Ferguson
Patricia Leitch
Christine Pullein-Thompson

A summer without horses
Broken horse
Corey in the saddle

Anthony Buckeridge Humour School

Richmal Crompton
Gillian Cross
George Layton

Jan Mark
Jean Ure

Jennings goes to school
Jennings as usual

Angela Bull

Historical: Victorian

5-7

Vivien Alcock
Clare Bevan
Frances Hodgson Burnett

Eileen Dunlop
Jennifer Carswell Hynd

Up the attic stairs
A patchwork of ghosts
The shadows of Owlsnap

Frances Hodgson Burnett

Family   Historical: Victorian

Angela Bull
Susan M Coolidge
Elizabeth Goudge

E Nesbit
Philippa Pearce
Alison Uttley

A little princess
The secret garden
Little Lord Fauntleroy

Sheila Burnford

Animals

W J Corbett
Colin Dann

Dodie Smith

Incredible journey

Betsy Byars

Family   Humour

12-14

Judy Blume
Paula Danziger
Louise Fitzhugh

Robin Klein
Lois Lowry
Thomas Rockwell

The cartoonist
Wanted Mud Blossom
The two thousand pound goldfish
The eighteenth emergency
The Blossoms saga
Midnight fox

Joanna Campbell
Pony/horse

8-11

Judith M Berrisford
Bonnie Bryant

Ruby Ferguson

Star of Shadowbrook Farm
Battle cry forever
Wonder's victory

Humphrey Carpenter
Magic School

Roy Apps
Terence Blacker
Gyles Brandreth
June Counsel
Pat Hutchins

Eva Ibbotson
Andrew Matthews
Jill Murphy
Chris Powling
J K Rowling

Mr Majeika
Mr Majeika and the ghost train
Mr Majeika and the school book week
Mr Majeika vanishes

Lewis Carroll
Fantasy

J M Barrie
Frank L Baum

Russell Hoban

Alice in Wonderland
Alice through the looking glass

Harriet Castor
Ballet

5-7

Jean Estoril
Lorna Hill

Antonia Barber

Pippa on pointe
Sadie's ballet school dream

Bob Cattell Sport

8-11

Rob Childs
Michael Coleman
Michael Hardcastle

Bill Naughton
Martin Waddell

World Cup fever
Bound for glory
The big test
Glory gardens

Aidan Chambers — Ghost/supernatural School Social issues

12-14

Jan Needle

Robert Westall

The present takers
Seal secret

Rob Childs — Sport

5-7

Terence Blacker
Tony Bradman
Bob Cattell
Michael Hardcastle

Bill Naughton
Diane Redmond
Martin Waddell

Soccer at Sandford
Football daft
Football fanatic
Football flukes
All goalies are crazy

John Christopher — Ghost/supernatural Science fiction

12-14

Nicholas Fisk
Douglas Hill

Maggie Prince

Tripods trilogy
Empty world

Beverly Cleary

Joyce Lancaster Brisley
Betsy Duffey
Louise Fitzhugh
Eve Garnett
Mary Hooper

Sheila Lavelle
Bel Mooney
Magdalen Nabb
Jacqueline Wilson

Ramona the pest
Ramona
Ramona forever
Ramona the brave

Michael Coleman

5-7

Terence Blacker
Malorie Blackman
Bob Cattell

Bruce Coville
Terrance Dicks

Shoot Dad
Cyber feud
Web trap

Susan M Coolidge

Louisa May Alcott
Elinor M Brent-Dyer
Frances Hodgson Burnett

L M Montgomery
Johanna Spyri
Laura Ingalls Wilder

What Katy did
What Katy did at school
What Katy did next

Susan Cooper

Adventure   Fantasy

12-14

8-11

Annie Dalton
Catherine Fisher
Alan Garner
Jenny Nimmo

Philip Pullman
J R R Tolkien
T H White

The Boggart
The Boggart and the monster
Seaward

Judy Corbalis

Family   Humour

Gyles Brandreth
June Counsel

Brough Girling
Robert Leeson

Wrestling princess and other stories
Oscar and the icepick

W J Corbett

Animals

Sheila Burnford
Colin Dann
Gerald Durrell

Kenneth Grahame
Brian Jacques
Rosalind Kerven

The song of Pentecost
Pentecost and the chosen one
Pentecost of Lickey Top

Alan Coren

Humour

Allan Ahlberg
Morris Gleitzman

Sid Fleischman

Arthur and the bellybutton diamond
Arthur the great detective

8-11

June Counsel

Fantasy   School

Humphrey Carpenter   Judy Corbalis

Dragon in class four
Dragon in spring term
Dragon in summer
Dragon in top class

Bruce Coville

Fantasy   Humour   Science fiction

Michael Coleman   B R Haynes
Mark Haddon   Douglas Hill

Aliens ate my homework
My teacher is an alien
My teacher fried my brains

Helen Cresswell

Adventure   Family   Fantasy

5-7

Joan Aiken   Diana Wynne Jones
Nina Beachcroft   Penelope Lively
Rachel Dixon   Philippa Pearce
Penelope Farmer   Catherine Storr

Bag of bones
Stonestruck
Moondial
Bagthorpe saga
Lizzie Dripping

Richmal Crompton

Family   Humour   School

Anthony Buckeridge   George Layton
Paul Jennings   Thomas Rockwell

Just William
William at war
Sweet William

Gillian Cross

Adventure   Family   School

12-14

Malorie Blackman
Judy Blume
Anthony Buckeridge
Rosa Guy

Gene Kemp
Jan Mark
Ruth Thomas
Jacqueline Wilson

The demon headmaster
The great elephant chase
Save our school

Kevin Crossley-Holland

Family   Mythology

Joan Aiken
Julian Atterton
Toby Forward
Alan Garner
Grace Hallworth

Cynthia Harnett
Terry Jones
Rosalind Kerven
Michael Morpurgo
T H White

Storm
Tales from the Mabinogian
Green children

Roald Dahl

Humour

5-7

Willis Hall
Anthony Horowitz

Eva Ibbotson

Charlie and the chocolate factory
Matilda
The BFG

Annie Dalton

Family   Fantasy

12-14

Vivien Alcock
Susan Cooper

Catherine Fisher
Toby Forward

The afterdark princess
The alpha box
Swan sister

Lucy Daniels — Animals

Brenda Jobling
Dick King-Smith
Tessa Krailing

Jenny Oldfield
Diane Redmond

Lion by the lake
Kitten in the kitchen
Mouse magic

Colin Dann — Adventure   Animals

Sheila Burnford
W J Corbett
Gerald Durrell
Kenneth Grahame
Brian Jacques

Rosalind Kerven
Dick King-Smith
Hugh Lofting
Dodie Smith
Joyce Stranger

Animals of Farthing Wood
King of the vagabonds
Beachdogs
The city cats

Paula Danziger — Family   Humour

12-14

Judy Blume
Betsy Byars
Anne Fine
Mary Hooper

Lois Lowry
Bel Mooney
Francesca Simon

Make like a tree and leave
Not for a million gazillion dollars
There's a bat in bunk five
Goodbye Harold Square
Earth to Matthew
Amber Brown is not a crayon

Andrew Davies

Humour   War 1939-45

Hunter Davies
Judith Kerr
Hilary McKay

Michael Morpurgo
Alison Prince
Ann Turnbull

Conrad's war
Educating Marmalade
Marmalade hits the big time

Hunter Davies

Humour

Andrew Davies
Willis Hall
Sheila Lavelle

Hilary McKay
Mary Rodgers

Flossie Teacake's fur coat
Flossie Teacake again
Flossie Teacake wins the lottery

Terry Deary

Historical: Tudor   School

5-7

Ann Jungman

Robert Leeson

The Lambton worm
The Grott Street Gang
The prince of rags and patches

Monica Dickens

Pony/horse

Bonnie Bryant
Wendy Douthwaite

K M Peyton
Christine Pullein-Thompson

Follyfoot
The horses of Follyfoot
New arrival at Follyfoot

8-11

8-11

Terrance Dicks — Science fiction

5-7

Tony Bradman
Gyles Brandreth
Michael Coleman

Nicholas Fisk
Douglas Hill

*The Wollagong incident
Cyberspace adventure
Virtual unreality*

Anne Digby — School

Enid Blyton
Elinor M Brent-Dyer

Mary Hooper
Ann M Martin

*First term at Trebizon
More trouble at Trebizon*

Franklin W Dixon — Adventure

Enid Blyton
Carolyn Keene

Fiona Kelly
Ann M Martin

*Hardy boys: River rats
Hardy boys: The desert thieves*

Rachel Dixon — Fantasy   Ghost/supernatural

Vivien Alcock
Helen Cresswell

Catherine Sefton

*The demon piano
The marshmallow experiment
The witch's ring*

Berlie Doherty

Family   Historical

Nina Bawden
Anne Fine

Penelope Lively
Philippa Pearce

Children of winter
Granny was a buffer girl
Willa and old Miss Annie

Wendy Douthwaite

Pony/horse

Judith M Berrisford
Bonnie Bryant

Monica Dickens
Christine Pullein-Thompson

The lost pony
Polly on location
The orange pony
Dream pony

Betsy Duffey

Animals   Humour   School

Beverly Cleary
Rose Impey

Lois Lowry

A boy in the doghouse
How to be cool in junior school
Lucky on the loose

Eileen Dunlop

Adventure   Family

Angela Bull
Monica Furlong
Jennifer Carswell Hynd

Garry Kilworth
Rosemary Sutcliff

Finn's island
Finn's Roman fort
Fatal error

Gerald Durrell — Animals

W J Corbett
Colin Dann

Dodie Smith
Joyce Stranger

The donkey rustlers
The talking parcel

Jean Estoril — Ballet Stage

Antonia Barber
Harriet Castor
Lorna Hill

Mal Lewis Jones
Noel Streatfield

Drina ballerina
Drina dances again
Drina dances in New York

Penelope Farmer — Fantasy

Nina Beachcroft
Lucy M Boston
Helen Cresswell
Pauline Fisk
Penelope Lively

Anne Merrick
Philippa Pearce
Catherine Storr
Alison Uttley

Charlotte sometimes
Thicker than water
Castle of bone
The summer birds

Ruby Ferguson — Pony/horse

Judith M Berrisford
Bonnie Bryant
Joanna Campbell

Patricia Leitch
Christine Pullein-Thompson

Jill has two ponies
Challenges for Jill
Jill and the perfect pony

Anne Fine

Family Humour School
5-7 12-14

Bernard Ashley
Judy Blume
Paula Danziger
Berlie Doherty

Gene Kemp
Hilary McKay
Ann Pilling
Jacqueline Wilson

8-11

The angel of Nitshill Road
Bill's new frock
How to write really badly

Catherine Fisher

Fantasy
12-14

Susan Cooper
Annie Dalton
Alan Garner
Diana Wynne Jones

Garry Kilworth
Jenny Nimmo
Philip Pullman

Snow-walker's son
The empty hand
Fintan's Tower

Nicholas Fisk

Fantasy Science fiction
12-14

John Christopher
Terrance Dicks
Douglas Hill

Maggie Prince
Russell Stannard

Grinny
Trillions
Monster maker

Pauline Fisk

Adventure Fantasy

Penelope Farmer
Diana Wynne Jones

Anne Merrick

The beast of Whixall Moss
The tygerpool
Telling the sea
The depot of Whixall Moss

Louise Fitzhugh — Family School

Betsy Byars
Beverly Cleary

Lois Lowry
Mary Rodgers

Harriet the spy
Nobody's family is going to change

Sid Fleischman — Adventure Humour

Henrietta Branford
Alan Coren
Brough Girling

Margaret Mahy
Ian Strachan

The whipping boy
Jim Ugly
Midnight horse

Toby Forward — Adventure Fantasy

Kevin Crossley-Holland
Annie Dalton
Elizabeth Hawkins

Jennifer Carswell Hynd
Philip Ridley

Travelling backwards
Wyvern summer
Wyvern winter

Monica Furlong — Fantasy Historical: Medieval

Julian Atterton
Eileen Dunlop
Leon Garfield

Rosemary Sutcliff
Geoffrey Trease

Robin's country
A year and a day
Juniper
Wise child

Leon Garfield
Historical: Victorian

8-11

5-7 12-14

Monica Furlong
Cynthia Harnett
Rosemary Sutcliff

Geoffrey Trease
Henry Treece

December Rose
John Diamond
The apprentices
Stolen watch
Black Jack

Alan Garner
Fantasy

12-14

Susan Cooper
Kevin Crossley-Holland
Catherine Fisher
Diana Wynne Jones
C S Lewis

William Mayne
Philip Pullman
J R R Tolkien
T H White

The weirdstone of Brisingamen
Elidor
Moon of Gomrath
A bag of moonshine

Eve Garnett
Family

Joyce Lancaster Brisley

Beverly Cleary

The family from One End Street
Holiday at the Dew Drop Inn

Jamila Gavin
Family   Ghost/supernatural

5-7 12-14

Malorie Blackman
Adèle Geras
Rumer Godden

Grace Hallworth
Julia Jarman
Catherine Sefton

Grandpa Chatterji
I want to be an angel
Someone's watching, someone's waiting

Adèle Geras
Family   Fantasy   Humour

5-7 12-14

Jamila Gavin
Rumer Godden

Ann Jungman
Kaye Umansky

The Fantora family photographs
Fantora family files

Brough Girling
Humour

5-7

Gyles Brandreth
Judy Corbalis
Sid Fleischman
Willis Hall
Robert Leeson

Margaret Mahy
Ian Strachan
Kaye Umansky
David Henry Wilson

The banger and chips explosion
Vera Pratt and the bishop's false teeth
Black hole patrol

Morris Gleitzman
Family   Humour

12-14

Roy Apps
Alan Coren
Paul Jennings

Robin Klein
Philip Ridley
Nicholas Warburton

Blabbermouth
Stickybeak
Worrywarts
Bellyflop

Rumer Godden
Family

Elizabeth Goudge
Jamila Gavin

Adèle Geras

The diddakoi
The doll's house
Miss Happiness and Miss Flower
Premlata and the festival of lights

Elizabeth Goudge

Historical

Frances Hodgson Burnett   Rumer Godden

The runaways
The little white horse

Kenneth Grahame

Animals

W J Corbett   Hugh Lofting
Colin Dann   A A Milne
Dick King-Smith

The wind in the willows
Toad of Toad Hall

Rosa Guy

Adventure   Family   Friends

Malorie Blackman   Ruth Thomas
Gillian Cross

Paris Peewee and the big dog
Billy the Great
Edith Jackson

Mark Haddon

Humour   Space

Bruce Coville   Paul Jennings
B R Haynes   Philip Ridley

Agent Z goes wild
Titch Johnson, almost world champion
Agent Z and the penguin from Mars

Willis Hall · Humour

Roald Dahl
Hunter Davies
Brough Girling
Anthony Horowitz
Eva Ibbotson
Ann Jungman

Roger McGough
Margaret Mahy
Angela Sommer-Bodenburg
Kaye Umansky
David Henry Wilson

The last vampire
The inflatable shop
The vampire vanishes
Vampire strikes back

Grace Hallworth · Other lands

Kevin Crossley-Holland   Jamila Gavin

Cric Crac
Listen to this story
Mermaids and monsters

Dennis Hamley · Animals   Ghost/supernatural   War 1939-45

Jan Mark
Alison Prince

Jean Ure

The War and Freddy
Hare's choice
Railway phantoms

Michael Hardcastle · Sport

5-7

Terence Blacker
Bob Cattell
Rob Childs

Bill Naughton
Diane Redmond
Martin Waddell

Winning goal
Soccer captain
The away team

Cynthia Harnett

Julian Atterton
Kevin Crossley-Holland
Leon Garfield

Rosemary Sutcliff
Geoffrey Trease

The wool pack
Stars of fortune
The load of unicorn

Elizabeth Hawkins

Adventure   Ghost/supernatural

Toby Forward
Jennifer Carswell Hynd

Catherine Sefton

Runner
The maze
Sea of peril

B R Haynes

Humour

Bruce Coville

Mark Haddon

Teacher creature
Strange brew
Attack of the killer ants

Diana Hendry

Family   Fantasy   Social issues

Clare Bevan

J K Rowling

Harvey Angel
Harvey Angel and the ghost child
Kid Kibble

Douglas Hill

John Christopher
Bruce Coville
Terrance Dicks

Nicholas Fisk
Maggie Prince

Deathwing over Veynaa
Dragon charmer
Galactic warlord

Lorna Hill

Antonia Barber
Harriet Castor
Jean Estoril

Mal Lewis Jones
Noel Streatfield

A dream of Sadlers Wells
Veronica at the Wells

Nigel Hinton

Russell Hoban
C S Lewis

Mary Norton
Robert C O'Brien

Beaver Towers
The witch's revenge
The dangerous journey

Russell Hoban

Lewis Carroll
Nigel Hinton
C S Lewis

William Mayne
Mary Norton
Robert C O'Brien

The mouse and his child

Anne Holm

War 1939-45

12-14

Judith Kerr
Ian Serraillier

Robert Westall

I am David
The sky grew red

8-11

Mary Hooper

Humour   School

5-7 12-14

Beverly Cleary
Paula Danziger

Anne Digby
Jean Ure

First term
Park Wood on ice
Best friends worst luck

Anthony Horowitz

Adventure   Humour

Roald Dahl
Eva Ibbotson
Willis Hall

Paul Jennings
Philip Ridley

The falcon's malteser
The switch
Granny
Groosham Grange

Ted Hughes

Environment   Fantasy

Clive King

Robert C O'Brien

The iron man
The iron woman
How the whale became

Pat Hutchins

Adventure Humour School

8-11

Henrietta Branford
Humphrey Carpenter
Rose Impey

Sheila Lavelle
Jacqueline Wilson

The case of the Egyptian mummy
The Mona Lisa mystery

Jennifer Carswell Hynd

Adventure Fantasy Historical

Angela Bull
Eileen Dunlop
Toby Forward

Elizabeth Hawkins
Catherine Sefton

Flight of the ebony owl

Eva Ibbotson

Fantasy Ghost/supernatural Humour

Humphrey Carpenter
Roald Dahl
Willis Hall
Anthony Horowitz
Ann Jungman

Andrew Matthews
Jill Murphy
J K Rowling
Angela Sommer-Bodenburg
Kaye Umansky

Dial a ghost
The haunting of Hiram
The great ghost rescue
Which witch

Rose Impey

Family Humour

5-7

Betsy Duffey
Pat Hutchins
Sheila Lavelle

Ann Pilling
Jean Ure
Jacqueline Wilson

The revenge of the rabbit
Fireballs from hell
Girls' gang

Brian Jacques
8-11

Adventure Animals

12-14

W J Corbett
Colin Dann

Garry Kilworth
Robert C O'Brien

Redwall
Outcast of Redwall
Salamandastron

Julia Jarman

Family

5-7

Malorie Blackman

Jamila Gavin

The Jessame stories
The time-travelling cat
Ghost of Tantony Pig

Paul Jennings

Humour

12-14

Roy Apps
Richmal Crompton
Morris Gleitzman
Mark Haddon
Anthony Horowitz

Philip Ridley
Thomas Rockwell
Jeremy Strong
Nicholas Warburton
David Henry Wilson

The Gizmo
Sink the Gizmo
Come back Gizmo

Brenda Jobling

Animals

Lucy Daniels
Dick King-Smith
Tessa Krailing

Jenny Oldfield
Diane Redmond
Joyce Stranger

A fox cub named Freedom
Goose on the run
Pirate the seal

Pete Johnson
Ghost/supernatural

12-14

Allan Frewin Jones
Anthony Masters
Paul Stewart

R L Stine
Robert Swindells

Ghost dog
My friend's a werewolf

Allan Frewin Jones
Adventure   Family

Enid Blyton
Pete Johnson
Anthony Masters

Paul Stewart
Robert Swindells

The skull stone file
The weird eyes file

Diana Wynne Jones
Fantasy

12-14

Joan Aiken
Nina Beachcroft
Helen Cresswell
Catherine Fisher

Pauline Fisk
Alan Garner
Philip Pullman
J K Rowling

Charmed life
The lives of Christopher Chant
The ogre downstairs
Eight days of Luke

Mal Lewis Jones
Ballet

Jean Estoril
Lorna Hill

Noel Streatfield

Cassie at the ballet school
Ghost at the ballet school
New friends at the ballet school

Terry Jones Fantasy Mythology

8-11

Joan Aiken
Julian Atterton

Kevin Crossley-Holland

Fairy tales
Saga of Eric the Viking
Nicobobinus

Ann Jungman Humour

5-7

Terry Deary
Adèle Geras
Willis Hall

Eva Ibbotson
Angela Sommer-Bodenburg

Vlad the Drac
Vlad the Drac goes travelling
Lucy and the big bad wolf

Carolyn Keene Adventure

Enid Blyton
Franklin W Dixon
Fiona Kelly

Ann M Martin
Anthony Masters
Malcolm Saville

Clue of the broken locket
The message in the hollow tree
Clue of the tapping heels

Fiona Kelly Adventure

Enid Blyton
Franklin W Dixon
Carolyn Keene

Ann M Martin
Anthony Masters
Malcolm Saville

Poison
Box of tricks
Mystery weekend

Gene Kemp

Bernard Ashley
Gillian Cross
Anne Fine
Tessa Krailing

Hilary McKay
Jan Needle
Ruth Thomas
Nicholas Warburton

Just Ferret
The turbulent term of Tyke Tyler
The prime of the Tamworth Pig
Goosey Farm: Dog's journey

Judith Kerr

War 1939-45

Nina Bawden
Andrew Davies
Anne Holm
Michelle Magorian

Alison Prince
Ian Serraillier
Ann Turnbull
Robert Westall

When Hitler stole pink rabbit
A small person far away
The other way round

Rosalind Kerven

Animals   Environment   Mythology

W J Corbett
Kevin Crossley-Holland

Colin Dann
Clive King

Whoever heard of a vegetarian fox
Wild
Aladdin and other tales from the Arabian nights

Garry Kilworth

Adventure   Animals   Fantasy

Joan Aiken
Eileen Dunlop

Catherine Fisher
Brian Jacques

The phantom piper
The raiders
The Welkin Weasels: Thunder Oak
The gargoyle

Clive King

Adventure   Environment

Ted Hughes
Rosalind Kerven

Robert C O'Brien

Stig of the dump
The town that went south
Me and my million

8-11

Dick King-Smith

Animals   Family

5-7

Elisabeth Beresford
Lucy Daniels
Colin Dann
Kenneth Grahame
Brenda Jobling

Hugh Lofting
Jenny Oldfield
Dodie Smith
E B White

The sheep pig
The crowstarver
Saddlebottom
Magnus Powermouse
Ace
Mouse called Wolf

Robin Klein

Family   Humour   Space

12-14

Judy Blume
Betsy Byars

Morris Gleitzman

Halfway across the galaxy and turn left
Hating Alison Ashley
Dresses of red and gold
All in the blue unclouded weather

Tessa Krailing

5-7

Lucy Daniels
Brenda Jobling
Gene Kemp

Sheila Lavelle
Jean Ure

Petsitters club: Donkey rescue
A dinosaur called Minerva
Miranda and friends

Sheila Lavelle

5-7

Judy Blume
Beverly Cleary
Hunter Davies
Pat Hutchins
Rose Impey

Tessa Krailing
Lois Lowry
Hilary McKay
Jill Murphy
Mary Rodgers

My best fiend
Calamity with the fiend
The fiend next door

George Layton

Anthony Buckeridge
Richmal Crompton

Thomas Rockwell

The fib and other stories
The swap and other stories

Robert Leeson

5-7 12-14

Bernard Ashley
Judy Corbalis
Terry Deary
Brough Girling

Jan Mark
Jan Needle
Robert Westall

Genie on the loose
The third class genie
The last genie
Smart girls

Patricia Leitch
Pony/horse

Bonnie Bryant
Ruby Ferguson

Mary O'Hara
Christine Pullein-Thompson

8-11

Pony puzzle
The summer riders
Chestnut gold
Jump for the moon

C S Lewis
Fantasy

J M Barrie
Frank L Baum
Alan Garner
Nigel Hinton

Russell Hoban
Philip Pullman
J R R Tolkien

The lion, the witch and the wardrobe
Prince Caspian
The voyage of the Dawn Treader
The last battle

Penelope Lively
Adventure   Fantasy

5-7 12-14

Nina Beachcroft
Lucy M Boston
Helen Cresswell
Berlie Doherty

Penelope Farmer
William Mayne
Philippa Pearce

Astercote
Revenge of Samuel Stokes
The voyage of QV 66
House inside out

Hugh Lofting — Animals

Colin Dann

Dick King-Smith

Kenneth Grahame

The story of Doctor Dolittle
The voyages of Doctor Dolittle
Doctor Dolittle and the green canary

Lois Lowry — Family

12-14

Judy Blume

Louise Fitzhugh

Betsy Byars

Sheila Lavelle

Paula Danziger

Jean Ure

Betsy Duffey

Jacqueline Wilson

Anastasia Krupnik
All about Sam
Switcharound
Anastasia's chosen career

Roger McGough — Humour

Willis Hall

Andrew Matthews

Margaret Mahy

The great smile robbery
Stinkers ahoy
Stowaways

Hilary McKay — Family   Humour

Andrew Davies

Sheila Lavelle

Hunter Davies

Ann Pilling

Anne Fine

Jacqueline Wilson

Gene Kemp

The amber cat
Dog Friday
The exiles at home

Michelle Magorian

Family   War 1939-45

12-14

Nina Bawden
Judith Kerr
Alison Prince

Ian Serraillier
Ann Turnbull
Robert Westall

Goodnight Mr Tom
Back home

8-11

Margaret Mahy

Adventure   Family   Humour

12-14

Sid Fleischman
Brough Girling
Willis Hall
Roger McGough

Nicholas Warburton
Ursula Moray Williams
David Henry Wilson

The greatest show off earth
The birthday burglar and the very wicked headmistress
Tingle berries, Tuckertubs and Telephones
Blood and thunder adventure
The pirates' mixed up voyage

Jan Mark

Family   School

5-7 12-14

Bernard Ashley
Anthony Buckeridge
Gillian Cross

Dennis Hamley
Robert Leeson
Jan Needle

Nothing to be afraid of
Thunder and lightnings
The dead letter box

Ann M Martin

Adventure   Family

Anne Digby
Franklin W Dixon

Carolyn Keene
Fiona Kelly

Abby and the mystery baby
California girls
Babysitters at Shadow Lake

Anthony Masters

12-14

Enid Blyton
Pete Johnson
Allan Frewin Jones
Carolyn Keene

Fiona Kelly
Willard Price
Malcolm Saville
Robert Swindells

The channel tunnel mystery
The mystery of Bloodhound Island
Cloning me, cloning you

Andrew Matthews

Fantasy   Humour

Humphrey Carpenter
Eva Ibbotson
Roger McGough

Jeremy Strong
Kaye Umansky

Mallery Cox and his Viking socks
Wickedoz
Wickedoz and the dragons of Stonewade

William Mayne

Fantasy

Alan Garner
Russell Hoban

Penelope Lively

Cuddy
Midnight Fair
Hob and the goblins

Anne Merrick

Adventure   Fantasy

Penelope Farmer
Pauline Fisk

Philippa Pearce

Someone came knocking
Hannah's ghost

A A Milne
Animals

8-11

Elisabeth Beresford
Michael Bond

Kenneth Grahame

Winnie the Pooh
The house at Pooh Corner

L M Montgomery
Family

Louisa May Alcott
Susan M Coolidge

Johanna Spyri
Laura Ingalls Wilder

Anne of Green Gables
Anne of Avonlea
Anne of the Island

Bel Mooney
Family

12-14

Joyce Lancaster Brisley
Beverly Cleary
Paula Danziger

Magdalen Nabb
Francesca Simon

I don't want to
But you promised
It's not fair

Michael Morpurgo
Adventure   Historical

5-7 12-14

Kevin Crossley-Holland
Andrew Davies
Jenny Nimmo

Philippa Pearce
Robert Westall

Mr Nobody's eyes
The wreck of the Zanzibar
Robin of Sherwood
Why the whales came
Wartman
The ghost of Grannia O'Malley

Jill Murphy

Gyles Brandreth
Humphrey Carpenter
Eva Ibbotson

Sheila Lavelle
Kaye Umansky

Worst witch
A bad spell for the worst witch
The worst witch strikes again
Geoffrey Strangeways

Magdalen Nabb

Beverly Cleary
Bel Mooney

Francesca Simon

The enchanted horse
Josie Smith
Josie Smith at school

Bill Naughton

Terence Blacker
Bob Cattell
Rob Childs

Michael Hardcastle
Martin Waddell

The goal keeper's revenge and other stories
My pal Spadger

Jan Needle

Aidan Chambers
Gene Kemp

Robert Leeson
Jan Mark

The bully
The skeleton at school
The sleeping party

E Nesbit

8-11

Family   Fantasy

Lynne Reid Banks
Lucy M Boston

Frances Hodgson Burnett
Sylvia Waugh

The railway children
Five children and It
The phoenix and the carpet

Jenny Nimmo

Family   Fantasy

Vivien Alcock
Nina Beachcroft
Susan Cooper

Catherine Fisher
Michael Morpurgo
Philip Pullman

The snow spider
Emlyn's moon
The witch's tears
Griffin's castle
The stone mouse

Mary Norton

Adventure   Family   Fantasy

Lynne Reid Banks
Elisabeth Beresford
Nigel Hinton

Russell Hoban
P L Travers
Sylvia Waugh

The Borrowers
The Borrowers afield
The Borrowers afloat
Bedknobs and broomsticks

Robert C O'Brien

Environment   Fantasy

12-14

Nigel Hinton
Russell Hoban
Ted Hughes

Brian Jacques
Clive King

Mrs Frisby and the rats of Nimh
Z for Zachariah

8-11

Mary O'Hara — Pony/horse

Enid Bagnold   Anna Sewell
Patricia Leitch

My friend Flicka

Jenny Oldfield — Animals

Lucy Daniels   Dick King-Smith
Brenda Jobling

Skin and bone
Socks the survivor
Solo the homeless

Philippa Pearce — Adventure Fantasy

Nina Beachcroft   Penelope Farmer
Lucy M Boston   Penelope Lively
Frances Hodgson Burnett   Anne Merrick
Helen Cresswell   Michael Morpurgo
Berlie Doherty   Alison Uttley

Tom's midnight garden
The way to Sattin Shore
A dog so small

K M Peyton — Animals Historical Pony/horse

Enid Bagnold   Monica Dickens
Judith M Berrisford   Christine Pullein-Thompson

Edge of the cloud
Flambards
Poor badger
Froggett's revenge

Ann Pilling

Anne Fine   Hilary McKay
Rose Impey   Jacqueline Wilson

Henry's leg
Mother's daily scream
The big pink

Chris Powling

Gyles Brandreth   Humphrey Carpenter

The razzle-dazzle rainbow
The conker as hard as a diamond
Spook at the superstore

Willard Price

Anthony Masters   Arthur Ransome

Amazon adventure
Arctic adventure
Elephant adventure

Alison Prince
Family   Ghost/supernatural   War 1939-45

Andrew Davies   Michelle Magorian
Dennis Hamley   Ann Turnbull
Judith Kerr

How's business
Screw loose

Maggie Prince — Space

John Christopher
Nicholas Fisk

Douglas Hill
Russell Stannard

Memoirs of a dangerous alien
Pulling the plug on the universe

Christine Pullein-Thompson — Pony/horse

Enid Bagnold
Judith M Berrisford
Bonnie Bryant
Monica Dickens

Wendy Douthwaite
Ruby Ferguson
Patricia Leitch
K M Peyton

I rode a winner
Stolen ponies
A pony in distress

Philip Pullman — Adventure   Fantasy

12-14

Joan Aiken
Susan Cooper
Catherine Fisher
Alan Garner

Diana Wynne Jones
C S Lewis
Jenny Nimmo
J R R Tolkien

Count Karlstein, ride demon huntsman
The firework-maker's daughter
Clockwork

Arthur Ransome — Adventure

Enid Blyton
Willard Price

Malcolm Saville

Swallows and Amazons
Missee Lee
Pigeon post

84

Diane Redmond Animals Sport Stage

Rob Childs
Lucy Daniels
Michael Hardcastle

Brenda Jobling
Joyce Stranger

Animal alert
Curtain call
United

8-11

Philip Ridley Fantasy Humour

Toby Forward
Morris Gleitzman
Mark Haddon

Anthony Horowitz
Paul Jennings

Kaspar in the glitter
Meteorite spoon
Krindle krax
Scribble boy
Zinder zunder

Thomas Rockwell Humour

Betsy Byars
Richmal Crompton
Paul Jennings
George Layton

Mary Rodgers
Jeremy Strong
David Henry Wilson

How to eat fried worms
How to fight a girl
How to get fabulously rich

Mary Rodgers Family Humour

Hunter Davies
Louise Fitzhugh

Sheila Lavelle
Thomas Rockwell

Freaky Friday

J K Rowling

8-11

Humphrey Carpenter   Diana Wynne Jones
Diana Hendry   Kaye Umansky
Eva Ibbotson

Harry Potter and the philosopher's stone
Harry Potter and the chamber of secrets

Malcolm Saville

Adventure

Enid Blyton   Anthony Masters
Carolyn Keene   Arthur Ransome
Fiona Kelly

Mystery at Witch End
The neglected mountain
Sea Witch comes home

Catherine Sefton

Adventure   Ghost/supernatural

5-7

Rachel Dixon   Elizabeth Hawkins
Jamila Gavin   Jennifer Carswell Hynd

In a blue velvet dress
Haunting of Ellen
Emer's ghost

Ian Serraillier

War 1939-45

Anne Holm   Michelle Magorian
Judith Kerr   Robert Westall

The silver sword

86

Anna Sewell
Pony/horse

Enid Bagnold   Mary O'Hara

Black Beauty

8-11

Francesca Simon
Family   Humour

Bel Mooney   Jean Ure
Magdalen Nabb   David Henry Wilson

Horrid Henry strikes it rich
Horrid Henry's nits
Horrid Henry and the secret club

Barbara Sleigh
Animals   Fantasy   Magic

Dodie Smith   E B White

Carbonel
Jessamy
Carbonel and Calidor

Dodie Smith
Adventure   Animals

Sheila Burnford   Barbara Sleigh
Colin Dann   Joyce Stranger
Gerald Durrell   E B White
Dick King-Smith

One hundred and one dalmations
The midnight kittens
The starlight barking

Angela Sommer-Bodenburg — Humour

Willis Hall
Eva Ibbotson

Ann Jungman
Kaye Umansky

The little vampire
The little vampire and the wicked plot
The little vampire gets a surprise

Johanna Spyri — Family

Louisa May Alcott
Susan M Coolidge

L M Montgomery
Laura Ingalls Wilder

Heidi

Russell Stannard — Space

Nicholas Fisk

Maggie Prince

The time and space of Uncle Albert
Black holes and Uncle Albert
Uncle Albert and the quantum quest

Paul Stewart — Animals   Ghost/supernatural

Pete Johnson
Allan Frewin Jones

R L Stine
Robert Swindells

Beyond the Deepwoods
The wakening
The midnight hand

R L Stine — Horror

Pete Johnson

Paul Stewart

Welcome to the dead house
Night of the living dummy
Attack of the mutant

Catherine Storr

Fantasy   Ghost/supernatural

Helen Cresswell
Penelope Farmer

Ursula Moray Williams

Marianne dreams
Clever Polly and the stupid wolf
The mirror image ghost

Ian Strachan

Adventure   Humour

Sid Fleischman

Brough Girling

House of danger
Journey of one thousand miles
The upside-down world of Ginger Nutt
Wayne loves custard

Joyce Stranger

Animals

Colin Dann
Gerald Durrell
Brenda Jobling

Diane Redmond
Dodie Smith

Simon's island
The secret of Hunter's keep

Noel Streatfield

Ballet   Family   Stage

Jean Estoril
Lorna Hill

Mal Lewis Jones

Ballet shoes
Caldicott Place
The circus is coming

Jeremy Strong — Humour

Allan Ahlberg
Tony Bradman
Henrietta Branford
Paul Jennings

Andrew Matthews
Thomas Rockwell
David Henry Wilson

Fatbag
The karate princess
My granny's great escape
Lightning Lucy

Rosemary Sutcliff — Historical: Medieval   Historical: Roman

5-7 12-14

Julian Atterton
Eileen Dunlop
Monica Furlong
Leon Garfield

Cynthia Harnett
Geoffrey Trease
T H White

Knight's fee
Witch's brat
The armourer's house

Robert Swindells — Adventure   Ghost/supernatural

12-14

Pete Johnson
Allan Frewin Jones
Anthony Masters

Paul Stewart
Robert Westall

Room 13
The outfit series
The ghosts of Givenham Keep
Jacqueline Hyde

Ruth Thomas

Malorie Blackman
Gillian Cross

Rosa Guy
Gene Kemp

The runaways
Hideaway
The secret

J R R Tolkien
Adventure   Fantasy

12-14

Susan Cooper
Alan Garner

C S Lewis
Philip Pullman

The Hobbit

P L Travers
Family   Fantasy   Humour

J M Barrie
Frank L Baum

Lucy M Boston
Mary Norton

Mary Poppins
Mary Poppins comes back
Mary Poppins in the park

Geoffrey Trease
Historical

12-14

Monica Furlong
Leon Garfield
Cynthia Harnett

Rosemary Sutcliff
Henry Treece

Bring out the banners
Cue for treason
The white knights of St Petersburg
Cloak for a spy
Curse on the sea

Henry Treece

Julian Atterton
Leon Garfield

Geoffrey Trease

The horned helmet
The Viking saga
Legions of the eagle

Ann Turnbull

Nina Bawden
Andrew Davies
Judith Kerr

Michelle Magorian
Alison Prince
Robert Westall

Pigeon summer
No friend of mine
Room for a stranger
A long way home

Kaye Umansky

5-7

Adèle Geras
Brough Girling
Willis Hall
Eva Ibbotson
Andrew Matthews

Jill Murphy
J K Rowling
Angela Sommer-Bodenburg
Jean Ure

Pongwiffy
Pongwiffy and the spell of the year
Pongwiffy and the pantomime

Jean Ure
Ballet   Family   Ghost/supernatural   School

5-7 12-14

Bernard Ashley
Anthony Buckeridge
Dennis Hamley
Mary Hooper
Rose Impey

Tessa Krailing
Lois Lowry
Francesca Simon
Kaye Umansky
Jacqueline Wilson

A proper little Nooryeff
Hey there super mouse
Wizard in the woods
Ghosts that lived on the hill

Alison Uttley
Historical

5-7

Lucy M Boston
Frances Hodgson Burnett

Penelope Farmer
Philippa Pearce

A traveller in time

Martin Waddell
Sport

5-7

Terence Blacker
Bob Cattell
Rob Childs

Michael Hardcastle
Bill Naughton

Napper goes for goal
Napper strikes again
Napper's luck

Nicholas Warburton
Humour

Paul Jennings
Morris Gleitzman

Gene Kemp
Margaret Mahy

You've been noodled
Climbing in the dark
Dennis Dip on Gilbert's pond

Sylvia Waugh
Adventure   Fantasy

Lynne Reid Banks
J M Barrie
Lucy M Boston

E Nesbit
Mary Norton

The Menyms
The Menyms in the wilderness
The Menyms under seige

Robert Westall
Adventure   War 1939-45

12-14

Aidan Chambers
Anne Holm
Judith Kerr
Robert Leeson
Michelle Magorian

Michael Morpurgo
Ian Serraillier
Robert Swindells
Ann Turnbull

The machine gunners
Blitz
Stormsearch
Creature in the dark

E B White
Animals

Dick King-Smith
Barbara Sleigh

Dodie Smith

Charlotte's web
Trumpet of the swan
Stuart Little

T H White
Fantasy   Mythology

Susan Cooper
Kevin Crossley-Holland

Alan Garner
Rosemary Sutcliff

Sword in the stone

8-11

Laura Ingalls Wilder Family

Louisa May Alcott
Susan M Coolidge

L M Montgomery
Johanna Spyri

The little house in the big woods
The little house on the prairie
On the banks of Plum Creek

Ursula Moray Williams Adventure   Animals   Fantasy

Margaret Mahy

Catherine Storr

Bogwoppit
Spid
Jeffy the burglar's cat
Adventures of the little wooden horse

David Henry Wilson Humour

Allan Ahlberg
Brough Girling
Willis Hall
Paul Jennings

Margaret Mahy
Thomas Rockwell
Francesca Simon
Jeremy Strong

Getting rich with Jeremy James
Elephants don't sit on cars
Gideon Gander solves the world's greatest mysteries

Jacqueline Wilson

5-7 12-14

8-11

Judy Blume
Beverly Cleary
Gillian Cross
Anne Fine
Pat Hutchins

Rose Impey
Lois Lowry
Hilary McKay
Ann Pilling
Jean Ure

The bed and breakfast star
The story of Tracy Beaker
The suitcase kid
The Lottie project
Bad girls
Double act

Authors for ages 12-14

Richard Adams
Animals   Fantasy

William Corlett
Brian Jacques

Terry Pratchett
J R R Tolkien

Watership Down
Plague dogs

12-14

Yinka Adebayo
Social issues

S E Hinton

Walter Dean Myers

Age ain't nothing but a number
Boyz to men
Livin' large

Joan Aiken
Ghost/supernatural   Historical
5-7 8-11

Vivien Alcock
Peter Carter
Ann Halam

Robin Jarvis
Diana Wynne Jones
Penelope Lively

Wolves of Willoughby Chase sequence
The Cockatrice boys
A creepy company
A bundle of nerves

Vivien Alcock
Ghost/supernatural   Science fiction
8-11

Joan Aiken
Lois Duncan

Ann Halam
Hugh Scott

The face at the window
The monster garden
The stonewalkers

Judy Allen
Other lands   Social issues

5-7

Bernard Ashley
Anita Desai
Paula Fox

Rosa Guy
Brian Jacques
Gary Paulsen

Highland quest
New York quest
Spanish quest

Rachel Anderson
Historical   Social issues   War

5-7

Michelle Magorian

Michael Morpurgo

Paper faces
The war orphan
Princess Jazz and the angels

Bernard Ashley
Family   Social issues

8-11

Judy Allen
Anne Fine
Alan Gibbons

Julie Johnston
Robert Leeson
Jan Mark

Dodgem
Janey
Johnnie's blitz
Running scared

Ros Asquith
Family   Humour   School

Yvonne Coppard
Paula Danziger

Josephine Feeney
Moya Simons

Bad hair day
Girls' gang
Keep fat class

Anne Bailey
Family   Social issues

Walter Dean Myers   Cynthia Voigt
Marilyn Sachs

Burn up
Breaking point
Cherie

Lynne Reid Banks
Social issues

8-11

Joan Lingard   James Watson

Broken bridge
One more river

Steve Barlow
Humour

Paula Danziger   Rosie Rushton

In love with an urban gorilla
Dream on!

Nina Bawden
Family

8-11

Tim Bowler   Ruth Elwin Harris
Theresa Breslin   Penelope Lively
Sharon Creech   Michelle Magorian
Adèle Geras   Mary Melwood
Rosa Guy   Billi Rosen

Grannie the Pag
The real Plato Jones

Lesley Beake
Social issues

Jean Craighead George   Beverley Naidoo
Frances Hendry

Song of Be
The strollers

12-14

James Berry — Other lands

Anita Desai   Kate Elizabeth Ernest

The future-telling lady
A thief in the village

Malorie Blackman — Family   Social issues
5-7 8-11

Betsy Byars   Jacqueline Roy
Peter Dickinson

Hacker
Not so stupid
Pig-heart boy

Judy Blume — Family   Romance   Social issues
8-11

Yvonne Coppard   Morris Gleitzman
Paula Danziger   Jacqueline Wilson

Deenie
Forever
Just as long as we're together
Tiger eyes

Tim Bowler — Family   Social issues

Nina Bawden   Geoffrey Trease
Katherine Paterson

River boy
Dragon's Rock
Shadows
Midget

Henrietta Branford

Historical: Medieval

5-7 8-11

Geraldine McCaughrean
Judith O'Neill

Rosemary Sutcliff
Jill Paton Walsh

Fire, bed and bone
The fated sky

Theresa Breslin

Family   Social issues

12-14

Nina Bawden
Sharon Creech
Berlie Doherty

Marilyn Sachs
Jill Paton Walsh

Different directions
Whispers in the graveyard
Kezzie
Death or glory boys
A homecoming for Kezzie

Melvin Burgess

Social issues

Aidan Chambers
Robert Cormier
Berlie Doherty
Anne Fine
Janni Howker

Angela Johnson
Robert Leeson
Robert Swindells
Paul Zindel

Junk
Loving April
The baby and the fly pie
The cry of the wolf
Burning Izzy
Angel for May

101

Betsy Byars
Family   Humour

8-11

Malorie Blackman   Katherine Paterson
Anne Fine   Jacqueline Roy
Rosa Guy

The summer of the swans
The Cybil war

Peter Carter
Historical   Social issues

Joan Aiken   Joan Lingard

Under Goliath
The hunted
The sentinels
The black lamp

Anne Cassidy
Family   Social issues   Thrillers

Robert Cormier   Berlie Doherty

Talking to strangers
In real life
The hidden child

Aidan Chambers
Social issues

8-11

Melvin Burgess   Cynthia Voigt
Robert Cormier

Breaktime
Dance on my grave
Now I know

John Christopher

Peter Dickinson
Nicholas Fisk
Lois Lowry

Andre Norton
Robert Swindells

A dusk of demons
Beyond the burning lands
The guardians

Susan Cooper

Fantasy

8-11

Catherine Fisher
Alan Garner
John Gordon
Monica Hughes

Robin Jarvis
Ursula Le Guin
J R R Tolkien

Dawn of fear
Over sea, under stone
The dark is rising

Yvonne Coppard

Family   Fantasy   Humour

Ros Asquith
Judy Blume
Paula Danziger
Josephine Feeney

Mary Hooper
Rosie Rushton
Moya Simons
Jacqueline Wilson

Not dressed like that, you don't!
Everybody else does! Why can't I?
Great! You've just ruined the rest of my life!

William Corlett

Fantasy

Richard Adams   Alan Garner

The magician's house series
The secret line

Robert Cormier Horror   Social issues   Thrillers

Melvin Burgess
Anne Cassidy
Aidan Chambers
Lois Duncan

Alan Durant
Pat Moon
James Watson
Paul Zindel

The middle of the night
The chocolate war
After the first death
We all fall down

12-14

Sharon Creech Family

Nina Bawden
Theresa Breslin
Gillian Cross
Ruth Elwin Harris

Michelle Magorian
Mary Melwood
Katherine Paterson

Chasing Redbird
Walk two moons

Gillian Cross Adventure

8-11

Sharon Creech
Alan Gibbons
Elizabeth Laird

Jan Mark
Katherine Paterson
Jean Ure

Born of the sun
Pictures in the dark
The iron way
Wolf

Annie Dalton Horror

8-11

Lois Duncan
Gwyneth Jones

Anthony Masters
Robert Westall

Naming the dark
Out of the ordinary
Night maze

Paula Danziger

8-11

Ros Asquith
Steve Barlow
Judy Blume

Yvonne Coppard
Mary Hooper
Rosie Rushton

The divorce express
Can you sue your parents for malpractice?
Thames doesn't rhyme with James

Marjorie Darke

Family   Historical

Elizabeth Laird
Julius Lester
Bette Paul

Mildred D Taylor
Theresa Tomlinson

A rose from Blighty
A question of courage
First of midnight
Comeback

Anita Desai

Other lands

Judy Allen
James Berry

Jamila Gavin
Frances Hendry

The village by the sea

Peter Dickinson

Adventure   Fantasy   Social issues

Malorie Blackman
John Christopher
Anthony Masters

James Watson
Robert Westall

Kin
Healer
The gift
Eva
The Changes series

12-14

105

Berlie Doherty

Family Social issues

8-11

Theresa Breslin
Melvin Burgess
Anne Cassidy

Robert Leeson
Geraldine McCaughrean
Pat Moon

Dear nobody
The snake stone
Street child

12-14

Ursula Dubosarsky

Family Social issues

Anne Holm

Robert Westall

The first book of Samuel
Bruno and the crumhorn
The white guinea-pig

Lois Duncan

Horror

Vivien Alcock
Robert Cormier
Annie Dalton

Ann Halam
Margaret Mahy
Hugh Scott

Stranger with my face
Don't look behind you
The eyes of Karen Connors

Alan Durant

Social issues Sport Thrillers

Robert Cormier
Paul Jennings
Pete Johnson

Anthony Masters
Sue Welford

Hamlet, bananas, and all that jazz
Blood
The good book
Publish or die
Leggs United

106

Michael Ende Fantasy

Brian Jacques
Terry Pratchett

Philip Pullman
J R R Tolkien

Momo
The neverending story

Kate Elizabeth Ernest Family   Other lands

12-14

James Berry
Virginia Hamilton

Errol Lloyd
Beverley Naidoo

Festus and Felix
Hope leaves Jamaica
Birds in the wilderness

Josephine Feeney Family   School

Ros Asquith

Yvonne Coppard

My family and other natural disasters
Truth, lies and homework

Anne Fine Family   School   Social issues

5-7 8-11

Bernard Ashley
Melvin Burgess
Betsy Byars
Julie Johnston
Robin Klein

Robert Leeson
Sue Townsend
Jean Ure
Jacqueline Wilson

Mrs Doubtfire
Step by wicked step
Flour babies
The Tulip touch

Catherine Fisher
Fantasy   Thrillers

8-11

Susan Cooper
Alan Garner
Robin Jarvis

Diana Wynne Jones
Ursula Le Guin
Philip Pullman

The candle man
Belin's Hill
The conjuror's game

Nicholas Fisk
Science fiction

8-11

John Christopher

Lois Lowry

Extraterrestrial tales
Pig ignorant
The worm charmers

Paula Fox
Social issues

Judy Allen
Julie Johnston

Cynthia Voigt

The gathering darkness
Monkey island

Leon Garfield
Ghost/supernatural   Historical

5-7 8-11

Philip Pullman

Jill Paton Walsh

The wedding ghost
Revolution!
Smith

12-14

Alan Garner

Susan Cooper
William Corlett
Catherine Fisher
John Gordon

Lesley Howarth
Diana Wynne Jones
Susan Price
Philip Pullman

Red shift
The owl service

Jamila Gavin

Anita Desai

Frances Hendry

The wheel of Surya
The eye of the horse
The track of the wind

Jean Craighead George

Lesley Beake
Judith O'Neill

Barbara Smucker

Julie of the wolves
Julie
My side of the mountain

Adèle Geras

Nina Bawden

Penelope Lively

The girls in the velvet frame
My grandmother's stories
Voyage
Silent snow secret snow

12-14

Alan Gibbons Social issues

Bernard Ashley   Robert Leeson
Gillian Cross

Street of the tall people
Ganging up
Some you win
Chicken

Morris Gleitzman Family Humour

8-11

Judy Blume   Moya Simons
Paul Jennings   Sue Townsend

Two weeks with the Queen
Bumface
The other facts of life

John Gordon Fantasy Ghost/supernatural

Alan Garner   Susan Cooper

Gilray's ghost
The giant under the snow
Midwinter witch

Rosa Guy Family

8-11

Judy Allen   Virginia Hamilton
Nina Bawden   Walter Dean Myers
Betsy Byars

The friends
The disappearance
The ups and downs of Carl Davis III

Ann Halam

Joan Aiken
Vivien Alcock

Lois Duncan

The fear man
The haunting of Jessica Raven
The powerhouse
Crying in the dark

Virginia Hamilton
Family

Kate Ernest

Rosa Guy

The magical adventures of Pretty Pearl
Zeely
The planet of Junior Brown

Ruth Elwin Harris
Family   Historical

Nina Bawden
Sharon Creech

Michelle Magorian
Mary Melwood

Beckoning hills
Beyond the orchid house
The silent shore

Frances Hendry
Historical

Lesley Beake
Anita Desai

Jamila Gavin

Chandra
Quest for a Queen
Quest for a maid
Quest for a kelpie

12-14

S E Hinton Social issues

Yinka Adebayo
Pete Johnson

Walter Dean Myers

Rumblefish
Tex
The outsiders

Anne Holm Social issues   War 1939-45

8-11

Ursula Dubosarsky
Hans Peter Richter
Robert Westall

Michael Morpurgo
Alick Rowe

I am David
The hostage

Mary Hooper Family   Romance

5-7 8-11

Yvonne Coppard
Paula Danziger

Millie Murray

The boyfriend trap
Mad about the boy

Lesley Howarth Environment   Family   Fantasy

Alan Garner

Bel Mooney

Maphead
Weather eye
The flower king

Janni Howker
Social issues

Melvin Burgess
Jan Mark

Robert Swindells

The nature of the beast
Isaac Campion
Badger on the barge

Monica Hughes
Fantasy   Science fiction

Susan Cooper
Gwyneth Jones
Louise Lawrence

Gillian Rubinstein
Robert Swindells

Sandwriter
The Isis pedlar
The dream catcher

12-14

Brian Jacques
Fantasy

8-11

Richard Adams
Judy Allen
Michael Ende

Robin Jarvis
Terry Pratchett
J R R Tolkien

Mariel of Redwall
Martin the warrior
The pearls of Lutra

Robin Jarvis
Fantasy

Joan Aiken
Susan Cooper
Catherine Fisher

Brian Jacques
Diana Wynne Jones

Tales for the Wyrd Museum
The Whitby witches
The Deptford histories

Paul Jennings

Ghost/supernatural Humour

8-11

Alan Durant
Morris Gleitzman

Moya Simons

Unreal!
Unmentionable!
The cabbage patch war

Angela Johnson

Social issues

Melvin Burgess
Julie Johnston

Marilyn Sachs

Humming whispers
Toning the sweep

Pete Johnson

Social issues

8-11

Alan Durant
S E Hinton

Robert Leeson
Jan Mark

Dead hour
The cool boffin
10 hours to live
Friends forever series

Julie Johnston

Social issues

Bernard Ashley
Anne Fine
Paula Fox

Angela Johnson
Jacqueline Roy

Hero of lesser causes
Adam and Eve and Pinch Me

12-14

114

Diana Wynne Jones

Fantasy   Science fiction

8-11

Joan Aiken
Catherine Fisher
Kenneth Lillington

Alan Garner
Robin Jarvis
Philip Pullman

Fire and hemlock
A tale of time city
Magicians of Caprona
Hexwood

12-14

Gwyneth Jones

Science fiction

Annie Dalton
Monica Hughes

Louise Lawrence

The hidden ones
Daymaker trilogy

Robin Klein

Family

8-11

Anne Fine
Marilyn Sachs

Cynthia Voigt

The listmaker
People might hear you
The sky in silver lace

Elizabeth Laird

Adventure   Family

Gillian Cross
Marjorie Darke

Jill Paton Walsh

Kiss the dust
Hiding out
Jay
Red sky in the morning

Louise Lawrence
Science fiction

Monica Hughes
Gwyneth Jones
Tamora Pierce

Susan Price
Gillian Rubinstein
Robert C O'Brien

The disinherited
Children of the dust
The road to Irriyan
Shadow of Mordican

Ursula Le Guin
Fantasy

Susan Cooper
Catherine Fisher
Tamora Pierce

Philip Pullman
J R R Tolkien

A wizard of Earthsea
The tombs of Atuan
Tehuna
The farthest shore

Robert Leeson
Family   Social issues

5-7 8-11

Bernard Ashley
Melvin Burgess
Berlie Doherty

Anne Fine
Alan Gibbons
Pete Johnson

It's my life
Red white & blue
Coming home
Jan alone
Grange Hill series

Julius Lester
Historical   Other lands

Marjorie Darke
Gary Paulsen

Mildred D Taylor

Two love stories
Long journey home

Kenneth Lillington Fantasy Humour

Diana Wynne Jones   Margaret Mahy

Isabel's double
Trick of the dark

Joan Lingard Social issues

5-7

Lynne Reid Banks   Elizabeth Lutzeier
Peter Carter   James Watson

Kevin and Sadie series
Maggie series
Tug of war
Hostages to fortune

Penelope Lively Historical

5-7 8-11

Joan Aiken   Adèle Geras
Nina Bawden

Going back
A stitch in time
The ghost of Thomas Kempe

Errol Lloyd Family

5-7

Kate Elizabeth Ernest   Millie Murray

In a strange land
Many rivers to cross

Lois Lowry Adventure Fantasy

8-11

John Christopher   Tamora Pierce
Nicholas Fisk   Jacqueline Wilson
Andre Norton

The giver

12-14

117

Elizabeth Lutzeier Social issues   War 1939-45

Joan Lingard   Billi Rosen
Hans Peter Richter

No shelter

12-14

Geraldine McCaughrean Historical

5-7

Henrietta Branford   Jill Paton Walsh
Berlie Doherty

A little lower than the angels
Plundering paradise
A pack of lies

Michelle Magorian Family   War 1939-45

8-11

Rachel Anderson   Ruth Elwin Harris
Nina Bawden   Mary Melwood
Sharon Creech

A spoonful of jam
A little love song
Cuckoo in the nest

Margaret Mahy Fantasy

8-11

Lois Duncan   Pat Moon
Kenneth Lillington   Bel Mooney

The changeover
The haunting
Dangerous spaces

Jan Mark

Family Social issues

5-7 8-11

Bernard Ashley
Gillian Cross

Janni Howker
Pete Johnson

Enough is too much already
Handles
The Hillingdon fox

Anthony Masters

Ghost/supernatural Thrillers

8-11

Annie Dalton
Peter Dickinson
Alan Durant

Hugh Scott
Sue Welford
Robert Westall

Raven
Roadkill
Nobody's child
Streetwise

Mary Melwood

Family Historical

Nina Bawden
Sharon Creech

Ruth Elwin Harris
Michelle Magorian

The watcher bee

Pat Moon

Social issues

5-7

Robert Cormier
Berlie Doherty
Margaret Mahy

Bette Paul
Barbara Smucker
Paul Zindel

Double image
The spying game
Nathan's switch

Bel Mooney
Ghost/supernatural   Historical   Social issues

8-11

Lesley Howarth   Margaret Mahy

The voices of silence
The stove haunting
Joining the rainbow

12-14

Michael Morpurgo
Historical   School   War 1939-45

5-7 8-11

Rachel Anderson   Alick Rowe
Anne Holm

Waiting for Anya
Friend or foe
War horse
War of Jenkins' ear

Millie Murray
Family   Social issues

Mary Hooper   Errol Lloyd

Sorrelle
Kiesha
Lady A, a teenage DJ

Walter Dean Myers
Social issues

Yinka Adebayo   Rosa Guy
Anne Bailey   S E Hinton

Somewhere in the darkness
Darnell Rock reporting
Scorpions

Beverley Naidoo
Other lands   Social issues

Lesley Beake   Robert Swindells
Kate Elizabeth Ernest

No turning back
Journey to Jo'burg
Chain of fire

12-14

Andre Norton
Science fiction

John Christopher   Gillian Rubinstein
Lois Lowry

Flight in Yiktor

Robert C O'Brien
War

8-11

Louise Lawrence   Robert Swindells

Z for Zachariah

Judith O'Neill
Historical

Jean Craighead George   Henrietta Branford

So far from Skye
Deep water

Katherine Paterson
Family

Tim Bowler   Gillian Cross
Betsy Byars   Cynthia Voigt
Sharon Creech

Bridge to Terabithia
Park's quest
Lyddie
Flip flop girl
Come sing Jimmy Jo

121

Bette Paul

12-14

Family

Marjorie Darke
Pat Moon
Barbara Smucker

Mildred D Taylor
Cynthia Voigt

Becca's race
Variations on a dream
Ladlass

Gary Paulsen

Historical

Judy Allen
Julius Lester

Mildred D Taylor

Nightjohn
Sarny
The Schernoff discoveries

Tamora Pierce

Fantasy

Louise Lawrence
Ursula Le Guin

Lois Lowry
Susan Price

Alanna, the first adventure
Wolf-speaker
Wild magic

Terry Pratchett

Fantasy

Richard Adams
Michael Ende

Brian Jacques
J R R Tolkien

The carpet people
Johnny and the dead
Truckers

Susan Price Fantasy

Alan Garner
Louise Lawrence

Tamora Pierce

The ghost drum
The bone dog
Forbidden doors

Philip Pullman Fantasy

8-11

Michael Ende
Catherine Fisher
Leon Garfield
Alan Garner

Diana Wynne Jones
Ursula Le Guin
J R R Tolkien

His dark materials series
Broken bridge
Ruby in the smoke

Hans Peter Richter War

Anne Holm
Elizabeth Lutzeier

Billi Rosen
Alick Rowe

Friedrich
I was there

Billi Rosen Historical   War

Nina Bawden
Elizabeth Lutzeier
Hans Peter Richter

Alick Rowe
Jill Paton Walsh

Andi's war
The other side of the mountain
A swallow in winter

Alick Rowe War

Anne Holm
Michael Morpurgo

Hans Peter Richter
Billi Rosen

Voices of danger
The panic wall

Jacqueline Roy Family

Malorie Blackman
Betsy Byars

Julie Johnston

A daughter like me
Fat chance
Playing it cool

Gillian Rubinstein Science fiction

Monica Hughes
Louise Lawrence

Andre Norton

Pure chance
Galax arena

Rosie Rushton Family   Humour

Steve Barlow
Yvonne Coppard

Paula Danziger

How could you do this to me, Mum?
I think I'll just curl up and die
Just don't make a scene, Mum!

Marilyn Sachs Family

Anne Bailey
Theresa Breslin

Angela Johnson
Robin Klein

Circles
The Golden Gates murders
Just like a friend

12-14

Hugh Scott Horror

Vivien Alcock
Lois Duncan

Anthony Masters
Robert Westall

Why weeps the Brogan?
Something watching

Moya Simons Family   Humour

Ros Asquith
Yvonne Coppard

Morris Gleitzman
Paul Jennings

Sit down Mum, there's something I've got to tell you
Hatty's hotline
Dead worried

Barbara Smucker Family   Other lands

Pat Moon
Bette Paul

Mildred D Taylor
Jean Craighead George

Underground to Canada
The Amish adventure

Rosemary Sutcliff

Henrietta Branford   Geoffrey Trease

Eagle of the ninth
The lantern bearers
Flame coloured taffeta

Robert Swindells

Science fiction   Social issues

8-11

Melvin Burgess   Monica Hughes
John Christopher   Beverley Naidoo
Janni Howker   Robert C O'Brien

Brother in the land
Daz 4 Zoe
Hydra
Follow a shadow
Stone cold

Mildred D Taylor

Historical   Other lands

Marjorie Darke   Gary Paulsen
Julius Lester   Barbara Smucker
Bette Paul

Let the circle be unbroken
Roll of thunder, hear my cry
Road to Memphis

J R R Tolkien

Fantasy

8-11

Richard Adams   Ursula Le Guin
Susan Cooper   Terry Pratchett
Michael Ende   Philip Pullman
Brian Jacques

Lord of the rings

Theresa Tomlinson
Family   Historical

Marjorie Darke   Jill Paton Walsh

The forestwife
The herring girls
The rope carrier

Sue Townsend
Humour

12-14

Anne Fine   Jacqueline Wilson
Morris Gleitzman

The growing pains of Adrian Mole
The secret diary of Adrian Mole aged 13³/₄

Geoffrey Trease
Adventure   Historical

8-11

Tim Bowler   Jill Paton Walsh
Rosemary Sutcliff

The Arpino assignment
The Calabrian quest
Song for a tattered flag

Jean Ure
Fantasy   Social issues

5-7 8-11

Gillian Cross   Jacqueline Wilson
Anne Fine

Plague 99
Skinny Melon and me
Love is forever

Cynthia Voigt

Anne Bailey
Aidan Chambers
Paula Fox

Robin Klein
Katherine Paterson
Bette Paul

Come a stranger
The runner

12-14

Jill Paton Walsh
Historical

5-7

Henrietta Branford
Theresa Breslin
Leon Garfield
Elizabeth Laird

Geraldine McCaughrean
Billi Rosen
Theresa Tomlinson
Geoffrey Trease

Grace
Fireweed
Parcel of patterns

James Watson
Social issues   Thrillers

Lynne Reid Banks
Robert Cormier

Peter Dickinson
Joan Lingard

The freedom tree
Talking in whispers

Sue Welford
Ghost/supernatural   Thrillers

Alan Durant
Anthony Masters

Robert Westall

Dreamstalker
Ghost in the mirror
Starlight city

Robert Westall

12-14

Adventure   Fantasy   Horror   Thrillers

8-11

Annie Dalton
Peter Dickinson
Ursula Dubosarsky
Anne Holm

Anthony Masters
Sue Welford
Hugh Scott

Blitzcat
The wind eye
Yaxley's cat

Jacqueline Wilson

Family   Romance

5-7 8-11

Judy Blume
Yvonne Coppard
Anne Fine

Lois Lowry
Sue Townsend
Jean Ure

Girls in love
Suitcase kid
Buried alive

Paul Zindel

Adventure   Social issues

Melvin Burgess
Robert Cormier

Pat Moon

Loch
Doom stone
The Pigman
The Pigman's legacy

Genres and themes

Adventure

5-7

Scoular Anderson
Malorie Blackman
Jon Blake
Gyles Brandreth
Jeff Brown
Lisa Bruce
Terrance Dicks
Andrew Donkin
Felicity Everett

Anne Forsyth
Sarah Garland
Brough Girling
Mick Gowar
Mary Hoffman
Julia Jarman
Margaret Joy
Ann Jungman

Robin Kingsland
Robert Leeson
Sam McBratney
Kara May
Marjorie Newman
Hilda Offen
Karen Wallace
Jacqueline Wilson

8-11

Joan Aiken
Roy Apps
Nina Bawden
Elisabeth Beresford
Terence Blacker
Malorie Blackman
Enid Blyton
Lucy M Boston
Tony Bradman
Gyles Brandreth
Henrietta Branford
Michael Coleman
Susan Cooper
Helen Cresswell
Gillian Cross
Colin Dann
Franklin W Dixon
Eileen Dunlop
Pauline Fisk

Sid Fleischman
Toby Forward
Rosa Guy
Elizabeth Hawkins
Nigel Hinton
Anthony Horowitz
Pat Hutchins
Jennifer Carswell Hynd
Brian Jacques
Allan Frewin Jones
Carolyn Keene
Fiona Kelly
Garry Kilworth
Clive King
Tessa Krailing
Robert Leeson
Penelope Lively
Margaret Mahy
Ann M Martin

Anthony Masters
Anne Merrick
Michael Morpurgo
Mary Norton
Philippa Pearce
Willard Price
Philip Pullman
Arthur Ransome
Malcolm Saville
Catherine Sefton
Dodie Smith
Ian Strachan
Robert Swindells
Ruth Thomas
J R R Tolkien
Sylvia Waugh
Robert Westall
Ursula Moray Williams

12-14

Gillian Cross
Peter Dickinson
Jean Craighead George

Elizabeth Laird
Lois Lowry
Geoffrey Trease

Robert Westall
Paul Zindel

Animals

5-7

Judy Allen
Heather Amery
Phyllis Arkle
Brian Ball
Jill Barklem
Alan Baron
Tony Bradman
Henrietta Branford
Damon Burnard
Harriet Castor
Kathryn Cave
Stan Cullimore
Terrance Dicks
P J Eastman
Anne Forsyth

Vivian French
Jane Gardam
John Gatehouse
Susan Gates
Adèle Geras
Margaret Gordon
Jana Novotny Hunter
Rose Impey
Anita Jeram
Ivan Jones
Tony Kerins
Dick King-Smith
Tessa Krailing
Arnold Lobel
James Marshall

E H Minarik
Pat Moon
Michael Morpurgo
Hiawyn Oram
Gillian Osband
Beatrix Potter
Shoo Rayner
Angie Sage
Rosemary Sutcliff
Jill Tomlinson
Alison Uttley
Jean Van Leeuwen
Martin Waddell
Colin West

8-11

Enid Bagnold
Elisabeth Beresford
Michael Bond
Sheila Burnford
W J Corbett
Lucy Daniels
Colin Dann
Betsy Duffey
Gerald Durrell
Kenneth Grahame

Dennis Hamley
Brian Jacques
Brenda Jobling
Gene Kemp
Rosalind Kerven
Garry Kilworth
Dick King-Smith
Tessa Krailing
Hugh Lofting
A A Milne

Jenny Oldfield
K M Peyton
Willard Price
Diane Redmond
Barbara Sleigh
Dodie Smith
Paul Stewart
Joyce Stranger
E B White
Ursula Moray Williams

12-14

Richard Adams

Ballet

8-11

Antonia Barber
Harriet Castor
Jean Estoril

Lorna Hill
Mal Lewis Jones

Noel Streatfield
Jean Ure

Environment

5-7

Jane Gardam

8-11

Ted Hughes
Rosalind Kerven
Clive King
Robert C O'Brien

12-14

Lesley Howarth

Family

5-7

Joy Allen
Rachel Anderson
Brian Ball
Ruskin Bond
Franz Brandenberg
Angela Bull
Ann Cameron
Dick Cate
Stan Cullimore
Terrance Dicks

Carolyn Dinan
Dorothy Edwards
John Escott
Anne Forsyth
Jane Gardam
Jamila Gavin
Adèle Geras
Michael Hardcastle
Mary Hooper
Shirley Hughes

Rose Impey
Thelma Lambert
Rob Lewis
Joan Lingard
Penelope Lively
Errol Lloyd
Hilda Offen
Ann Pilling
Pat Thomson

Family (cont)

8-11

Allan Ahlberg
Joan Aiken
Vivien Alcock
Louisa May Alcott
Bernard Ashley
Lynne Reid Banks
Nina Bawden
Clare Bevan
Judy Blume
Michael Bond
Lucy M Boston
Joyce Lancaster
    Brisley
Frances Hodgson
    Burnett
Betsy Byars
Beverly Cleary
Susan M Coolidge
Judy Corbalis
Helen Cresswell
Richmal Crompton
Gillian Cross

Kevin Crossley-Holland
Annie Dalton
Paula Danziger
Berlie Doherty
Eileen Dunlop
Anne Fine
Louise Fitzhugh
Eve Garnett
Jamila Gavin
Adèle Geras
Morris Gleitzman
Rumer Godden
Rosa Guy
Diana Hendry
Rose Impey
Julia Jarman
Allan Frewin Jones
Dick King-Smith
Tessa Krailing
Sheila Lavelle
Lois Lowry
Hilary McKay

Michelle Magorian
Margaret Mahy
Jan Mark
Ann M Martin
L M Montgomery
Bel Mooney
Magdalen Nabb
E Nesbit
Jenny Nimmo
Mary Norton
Ann Pilling
Alison Prince
Mary Rodgers
Francesca Simon
Johanna Spyri
Noel Streatfield
P L Travers
Ann Turnbull
Jean Ure
Laura Ingalls Wilder
Jacqueline Wilson

12-14

Bernard Ashley
Ros Asquith
Anne Bailey
Nina Bawden
Malorie Blackman
Judy Blume
Tim Bowler
Theresa Breslin
Betsy Byars
Anne Cassidy
Yvonne Coppard
Sharon Creech
Paula Danziger
Marjorie Darke
Berlie Doherty

Ursula Dubosarsky
Kate Elizabeth Ernest
Josephine Feeney
Anne Fine
Morris Gleitzman
Rosa Guy
Virginia Hamilton
Ruth Elwin Harris
Mary Hooper
Lesley Howarth
Robin Klein
Elizabeth Laird
Robert Leeson
Errol Lloyd
Michelle Magorian

Jan Mark
Mary Melwood
Millie Murray
Katherine Paterson
Bette Paul
Jacqueline Roy
Rosie Rushton
Marilyn Sachs
Moya Simons
Barbara Smucker
Theresa Tomlinson
Cynthia Voigt
Jacqueline Wilson

Fantasy

5-7

Joan Aiken
Margaret Stuart Barry
Terence Blacker
Tony Bradman
Jeff Brown
Patrick Skene Catling
Kathryn Cave

Helen Cresswell
Anne Fine
Anne Forsyth
Florence Parry Heide
Douglas Hill
Mary Hoffman

Robert Leeson
Helen Muir
Marjorie Newman
Ann Ruffell
Kaye Umansky
Jill Paton Walsh

8-11

Allan Ahlberg
Joan Aiken
Vivien Alcock
Lynne Reid Banks
J M Barrie
Frank L Baum
Nina Beachcroft
Elisabeth Beresford
Clare Bevan
Lucy M Boston
Tony Bradman
Gyles Brandreth
Lewis Carroll
Susan Cooper
June Counsel
Bruce Coville
Helen Cresswell
Annie Dalton
Rachel Dixon
Penelope Farmer

Catherine Fisher
Nicholas Fisk
Pauline Fisk
Toby Forward
Monica Furlong
Alan Garner
Adèle Geras
Diana Hendry
Nigel Hinton
Russell Hoban
Ted Hughes
Jennifer Carswell Hynd
Eva Ibbotson
Diana Wynne Jones
Terry Jones
Garry Kilworth
Robert Leeson
C S Lewis
Penelope Lively

Andrew Matthews
William Mayne
Anne Merrick
Jill Murphy
E Nesbit
Jenny Nimmo
Mary Norton
Robert C O'Brien
Philippa Pearce
Philip Pullman
Philip Ridley
J K Rowling
Barbara Sleigh
Catherine Storr
J R R Tolkien
P L Travers
Sylvia Waugh
T H White
Ursula Moray Williams

12-14

Richard Adams
Susan Cooper
Yvonne Coppard
William Corlett
Peter Dickinson
Michael Ende
Catherine Fisher
Alan Garner
John Gordon

Lesley Howarth
Monica Hughes
Brian Jacques
Robin Jarvis
Diana Wynne Jones
Ursula Le Guin
Kenneth Lillington
Lois Lowry

Margaret Mahy
Tamora Pierce
Terry Pratchett
Susan Price
Philip Pullman
J R R Tolkien
Jean Ure
Robert Westall

Ghost/supernatural

5-7

Eleanor Allen
Jon Blake

Andrew Donkin
Jana Novotny Hunter

Catherine Sefton
Jill Paton Walsh

8-11

Vivien Alcock
Aidan Chambers
John Christopher
Rachel Dixon
Jamila Gavin
Dennis Hamley

Elizabeth Hawkins
Eva Ibbotson
Pete Johnson
Anthony Masters
Alison Prince

Catherine Sefton
Paul Stewart
Catherine Storr
Robert Swindells
Jean Ure

12-14

Joan Aiken
Vivien Alcock
Leon Garfield

John Gordon
Ann Halam
Paul Jennings

Anthony Masters
Bel Mooney
Sue Welford

Genres

Historical

5-7

Joan Aiken
Leon Garfield
Mick Gowar

Mary Hooper
Michael Lawrence

Michael Morpurgo
Jill Paton Walsh

8-11

Julian Atterton m
Antonia Barber
Angela Bull m
Frances Hodgson
   Burnett v
Terry Deary t

Berlie Doherty
Monica Furlong m
Leon Garfield v
Elizabeth Goudge
Cynthia Harnett m
Jennifer Carswell Hynd

Michael Morpurgo
K M Peyton
Rosemary Sutcliff m r
Geoffrey Trease
Henry Treece
Alison Uttley

12-14

Joan Aiken
Rachel Anderson
Henrietta Branford m
Peter Carter
Marjorie Darke
Leon Garfield
Jamila Gavin
Adèle Geras

Ruth Elwin Harris
Frances Hendry
Julius Lester
Penelope Lively
Geraldine McCaughrean
Mary Melwood
Bel Mooney
Michael Morpurgo

Judith O'Neill
Gary Paulsen
Billi Rosen
Rosemary Sutcliff
Mildred D Taylor
Theresa Tomlinson
Geoffrey Trease
Jill Paton Walsh

m Medieval
r Roman
t Tudor
v Victorian

Genres

Horror

8-11

R L Stine

12-14

Robert Cormier
Annie Dalton
Lois Duncan
Ann Halam
Hugh Scott
Robert Westall

Humour

5-7

Allan Ahlberg
Jonathan Allen
Joy Allen
Judy Allen
Linda Allen
Heather Amery
Scoular Anderson
Laurence Anholt
Brian Ball
Alan Baron
Margaret Stuart Barry
S & J Berenstein
Terence Blacker
Jon Blake
Michael Bond
Tony Bradman
Franz Brandenberg
Gyles Brandreth
Henrietta Branford
Jeff Brown
Keith Brumpton
Janet Burchett &
   Sarah Vogler
Nick Butterworth
Harriet Castor

Dick Cate
Patrick Skene Catling
Kathryn Cave
Bennett Cerf
Michael Coleman
June Crebbin
Helen Cresswell
Stan Cullimore
John Cunliffe
Roald Dahl
Terry Deary
Terrance Dicks
P J Eastman
Dorothy Edwards
Vivian French
John Gatehouse
Brough Girling
Mick Gowar
Colin & Jacqui Hawkins
Sarah Hayes
Syd Hoff
Mary Hoffman
Mary Hooper
Shirley Hughes
Rose Impey

Anita Jeram
Ivan Jones
Ann Jungman
Tony Kerins
Dick King-Smith
Robin Kingsland
Thelma Lambert
Sheila Lavelle
Theo Le Sieg
Robert Leeson
Rob Lewis
Penelope Lively
Arnold Lobel
Sam McBratney
Alexander McCall-
   Smith
Geraldine McCaughrean
Jan Mark
James Marshall
Kara May
E H Minarik
Pat Moon
Michael Morpurgo
Helen Muir
Margaret Nash

Humour (cont)

5-7 (cont)

Marjorie Newman
Hiawyn Oram
Gillian Osband
Ann Pilling
Chris Powling
Alf Proysen
Shoo Rayner
Frank Rodgers
Gerald Rose
Ann Ruffell

John Ryan
Margaret Ryan
Angie Sage
Catherine Sefton
Dr Seuss
Dyan Sheldon
Pat Thomson
Ross Thomson
Jill Tomlinson

Hazel Townson
Kaye Umansky
Jean Van Leeuwen
Max Velthuijs
Martin Waddell
Karen Wallace
Colin West
Bob Wilson
Jacqueline Wilson

8-11

Allan Ahlberg
Roy Apps
Terence Blacker
Judy Blume
Tony Bradman
Gyles Brandreth
Henrietta Branford
Joyce Lancaster
  Brisley
Anthony Buckeridge
Betsy Byars
Judy Corbalis
Alan Coren
Bruce Coville
Richmal Crompton
Roald Dahl
Paula Danziger
Andrew Davies
Hunter Davies
Betsy Duffey
Anne Fine

Sid Fleischman
Adèle Geras
Brough Girling
Morris Gleitzman
Mark Haddon
Willis Hall
B R Haynes
Mary Hooper
Anthony Horowitz
Pat Hutchins
Eva Ibbotson
Rose Impey
Paul Jennings
Ann Jungman
Gene Kemp
Robin Klein
Sheila Lavelle
George Layton
Robert Leeson
Roger McGough

Hilary McKay
Margaret Mahy
Andrew Matthews
Jill Murphy
Jan Needle
Ann Pilling
Chris Powling
Philip Ridley
Thomas Rockwell
Mary Rodgers
Francesca Simon
Angela Sommer-
  Bodenburg
Ian Strachan
Jeremy Strong
P L Travers
Kaye Umansky
Nicholas Warburton
David Henry Wilson
Jacqueline Wilson

12-14

Ros Asquith
Steve Barlow
Betsy Byars
Yvonne Coppard

Morris Gleitzman
Paul Jennings
Kenneth Lillington

Rosie Rushton
Moya Simons
Sue Townsend

Magic

5-7

Jonathan Allen
Linda Allen
Margaret Stuart Barry
Terence Blacker
Gyles Brandreth
Patrick Skene Catling

Anne Fine
Philippa Gregory
Ann Jungman
Sheila Lavelle
Helen Muir

Alf Proysen
Ann Ruffell
Catherine Sefton
Kaye Umansky
Jean Ure

8-11

Humphrey Carpenter
Jill Murphy

Magdalen Nabb
J K Rowling

Barbara Sleigh
Kaye Umansky

Mythology

8-11

Julian Atterton
Kevin Crossley-Holland

Terry Jones
Rosalind Kerven

T H White

Other lands

8-11

Grace Hallworth

12-14

Judy Allen
James Berry
Anita Desai

Kate Elizabeth Ernest
Jean Craighead George
Julius Lester

Beverley Naidoo
Barbara Smucker
Mildred D Taylor

Pony/horse

8-11

Enid Bagnold
Judith M Berrisford
Bonnie Bryant
Joanna Campbell
Monica Dickens

Wendy Douthwaite
Ruby Ferguson
Patricia Leitch
Mary O'Hara

K M Peyton
Christine Pullein-
   Thompson
Anna Sewell

Romance

Genres

12-14

Judy Blume
Paula Danziger
Mary Hooper
Jacqueline Wilson

School

5-7

Brian Ball
Michael Coleman
Susan Gates

Margaret Joy
Robert Leeson
Wes Magee

Margaret Nash
Jean Ure

8-11

Bernard Ashley
Judy Blume
Enid Blyton
Elinor M Brent-Dyer
Anthony Buckeridge
Humphrey Carpenter
Aidan Chambers
Beverly Cleary
June Counsel

Richmal Crompton
Gillian Cross
Terry Deary
Anne Digby
Betsy Duffey
Anne Fine
Louise Fitzhugh
Mary Hooper
Pat Hutchins

Gene Kemp
Tessa Krailing
George Layton
Robert Leeson
Jan Mark
Jan Needle
J K Rowling
Jean Ure

12-14

Ros Asquith
Josephine Feeney

Anne Fine
Michael Morpurgo

Science fiction

5-7

Jon Blake

8-11

John Christopher
Bruce Coville
Terrance Dicks
Nicholas Fisk
Douglas Hill

12-14

Vivien Alcock
John Christopher
Nicholas Fisk
Monica Hughes
Diana Wynne Jones
Gwyneth Jones
Louise Lawrence
Andre Norton
Gillian Rubinstein
Robert Swindells

Genres

Social issues

8-11

Aidan Chambers
Diana Hendry

12-14

Yinka Adebayo
Judy Allen
Rachel Anderson
Bernard Ashley
Anne Bailey
Lynne Reid Banks
Lesley Beake
Malorie Blackman
Judy Blume
Tim Bowler
Theresa Breslin
Melvin Burgess
Peter Carter
Anne Cassidy
Aidan Chambers

Robert Cormier
Peter Dickinson
Berlie Doherty
Ursula Dubosarsky
Alan Durant
Anne Fine
Paula Fox
Alan Gibbons
S E Hinton
Anne Holm
Janni Howker
Angela Johnson
Pete Johnson
Julie Johnston

Robert Leeson
Joan Lingard
Elizabeth Lutzeier
Jan Mark
Pat Moon
Bel Mooney
Millie Murray
Walter Dean Myers
Beverley Naidoo
Robert Swindells
Jean Ure
Cynthia Voigt
James Watson
Paul Zindel

Space

8-11

Mark Haddon
Robin Klein
Maggie Prince
Russell Stannard

Genres

142

Sport

5-7

Janet Burchett &
    Sarah Vogler
Rob Childs
Michael Coleman

8-11

Terence Blacker
Tony Bradman
Bob Cattell
Rob Childs
Michael Coleman
Michael Hardcastle
Bill Naughton
Diane Redmond
Martin Waddell

12-14

Alan Durant

Stage

8-11

Antonia Barber
Jean Estoril
Diane Redmond
Noel Streatfield

Thrillers

12-14

Anne Cassidy
Robert Cormier
Alan Durant

Catherine Fisher
Anthony Masters
James Watson

Sue Welford
Robert Westall

War

8-11

Nina Bawden *
Andrew Davies *
Dennis Hamley *
Anne Holm *

Judith Kerr *
Michelle Magorian *
Alison Prince *

Ian Serraillier *
Ann Turnbull *
Robert Westall *

12-14

Rachel Anderson
Anne Holm *
Elizabeth Lutzeier *

Michelle Magorian *
Michael Morpurgo *
Robert C O'Brien

Hans Peter Richter
Billi Rosen
Alick Rowe

*1939-45

Series

This information supplied by Peters Library Service

Many children's books are published within series and this is often a helpful guide to finding similar authors.

Beginning to read series

Australian beginners

Beginner books (Collins)
Bodley Head beginners
Bright and early books

Classic collection (Collins)
Creepies
Critters of the night (US)

Disney's first readers level 1/ 2/ 3

Early step into reading (US)

First storybooks

Grandpa & Finley books

Happy families

I am reading
I can read (US)

Letterland reading at home
Little readers
Little stories (Ladybird)

My first I can read books (US)

Postman Pat beginner readers
Postman Pat beginners
Postman Pat easy readers

Read it yourself
Read together
Read with Ladybird: level 1/ 2/ 3
Read with Little Hippo
Ready, steady, read!
Red Fox beginners
Red nose collection
Red nose readers

Share a story
Spangles

Thomas easy-to read

Usborne castle tales
Usborne reading for beginners
Usborne rhyming stories

Easy readers series

A to Z mysteries (US)
Angels FC
Animal crackers
Animal heroes
Antelopes

Banana books
Best pets
Betsy Biggalow Caribbean stories

Blue bananas
Bunch of baddies

Cartwheels
Chillers
Clipper Street
Collins red storybooks
Collins yellow storybooks
Colour jets

Colour young Puffin
Computer whizzkidz
Corgi pups
Crackers
Crazy gang
Creakie Hall
Creepies

Derek the Depressed Viking
Dynamite Deela

First young Puffin
First stepping stone books (US)
Fizzy
Flippers
Frank N Stein stories
From the files of Police Dog 99...
Gator girls (US)
Gazelles
Ginger Ninja
Graffix

Historical storybooks
Houdini Club magic mysteries (US)

Invisible Ben stories

Jets
Jumbo jets
Jungle bunch

Kites

Little stories
Lizzie Green stories

Magic tree house (US)
Mona the Vampire

The one and only
Orchard crunchies
Orchard super crunchies

Pebbledown Bay
Pet pals

Piccadilly pips
Pirate adventure
Pleebus books
Postman Pat easy readers
Potbelly
Puffin read alone
Puzzle Planet adventures

Racers
Read alone (Hodder)
Read alones (Viking)

Seriously silly stories
Shivery storybooks
Shrinky kid stories
Skinny books (Australian series)
Sparks
Sprinters
Starring Henrietta
Step into reading (US series)
Stepping stone books (US)
Story books (Hodder)
Storybooks (Macdonald)

The Tigers
Tigers
Treetops
Tremors
Tui Turbo (New Zealand series)

Wizziwig

Yellow bananas
Young Hippo
Young Hippo Adventure
Young Hippo Animal
Young Hippo Funny
Young Hippo Magic
Young Hippo School
Young Hippo Spooky
Young Puffin read alones

Series

Novels

Adventure game books
Adventure! (Enid Blyton)
Adventures of Shirley Holmes
Adventures with Jeremy James (David Henry Wilson)
Adventurous four (Enid Blyton)
Andersen young reader's library
Andre Deutsch classics
Animal alert (Jenny Oldfield)
Animal Ark (Lucy Daniels)
Animal Ark pets (Lucy Daniels)
Animal alert (Jenny Oldfield)
Animal rescue squad (Ellen Weiss)
Animal sanctuary
Animorphs (K A Applegate)
Anywhere ring (US)
Are you afraid of the dark? (US)

Babysitters Club (Ann M Martin)
Babysitters mysteries (Ann M Martin)
Babysitters little sister (Ann M Martin)
Ballerinas (Harriet Castor)
Ballet School (Emily Costello)
Biggles (W E Johns)
Bonechillers (B R Haynes)
Bullseye chillers (US)

Café Club (Ann Bryant)
Cats of Cuckoo Square (Adèle Geras)
Chalet School (Elinor M Brent-Dyer)
City Limits (Bernard Ashley)
Comets
Computer game addict
Crabtree chronicles (Robin Kingsland)
Critters of the night (US)

Disney

Enid Blyton's adventure series
Epix

Famous Five (Enid Blyton)
Flashbacks
Ghosthunters (Anthony Masters)
Ghosts of Fear Street (R L Stine)

Give yourself goosebumps (R L Stine)
Goosebumps (R L Stine)
Glory Gardens (Bob Cattell)
Graveyard School

Hair-raisers (Margaret Clark) (Australia)
Happy days (Enid Blyton)
Hardy boys (Franklin W Dixon)
Hardy boys casefiles (Franklin W Dixon)
Hercules : the legendary journeys
Hippo adventure
Hippo animal
Hippo fantasy
Hippo funny
Hippo ghost
Hippo Hollywood
Hippo mystery
Hippo sport
Hollywell Stables (Samantha Alexander)
Home Farm twins (Jenny Oldfield)
Hunter and Moon mysteries (Allan Frewin Jones)

Internet Dectectives (Michael Coleman)
Ironfist Chinmi (Takeshi Maelawa)

Jackie (Judith M Berrisford)
Jennings (Anthony Buckeridge)
Jill (Ruby Ferguson)
Just William (Richmal Crompton)

Kelpies (Cannongate)
Leggs United (Alan Durant)
Lenny and Jake (Hazel Townson)
Leopard books (Scripture Union)
Little sister (Allan Frewin Jones)

Mammoth reads
Mammoth storybooks
Magic pony (Elizabeth Lindsay)
Melvin & the Deadheads (Roy Apps)
Midnight Dancer (Elizabeth Lindsay)
Mindwarp (Chris Archer)
Mystery (Enid Blyton)
Mystery and adventure (Enid Blyton)

Mystery Club (Fiona Kelly)
Mystery kids (Fiona Kelly)

Nancy Drew (Carolyn Keene)
Nancy Drew files (Carolyn Keene)
Newspaper kids (Juanita Phillips)

Orchard red apple
Oxford children's modern classics

Paddington storybooks (Michael Bond)
Pavilion classics
Petsitters Club (Tessa Krailing)
Police dog (Anthony Masters)
Polly (Wendy Douthwaite)
Pony Tails (Bonnie Bryant)
Puppy patrol (Jenny Dale)
Puffin classics
Puffin modern classics

Quirx

Racers (Walker)
Rainbow Animal Hospital (Steve Attridge)
Raven Hill mysteries (Emily Rodda)
Real adventures of Jonny Quest (Brad
    Quentin)
Riddles (Enid Blyton)
Riders (Samantha Alexander)
Riding Academy (Alison Hart) (US)
Rugrats

Saddle Club (Bonnie Bryant)
Sandy Lane Stables
Saturday Club (Jana Novotny Hunter)
Secret Seven (Enid Blyton)
Sheltie (Peter Clover)
Sister, sister (US)
Sleepover
Sleepover Club
Soccer mad (Rob Childs)
Spider-Man
Spook files
Spooksville (Christopher Pike)
Sprinters (Walker)
Stacey and friends (Allan Frewin Jones) (US)

Star Wars : galaxy of fear
Star Wars : young Jedi knights
Stepping stone books (US)
Story library (Kingfisher)
Strange matter
Suffers
Sweet Valley twins (Jamie Suzanne)
Sweet valley twins: Unicorn Club (Alice Nicole
    Johansson)
Swoppers

Tales from the crypt (US)
The fab four (Ros Asquith)
The kids in Miss Colman's class) (Ann Martin)
The Outfit (Robert Swindells)
The web
The Zack files (Dan Greenburg)
Tiger books (Scripture Union)
Time Rangers (Rob Childs)
Total football (Alan Gibbons)
Trophy Chapter Books (Australian series)
Tudor terror (Terry Deary)

Unexplained
Usborne spinechillers

Walker doubles
Walker read alones
Walker story books
We love animals (Jean Ure)
Weird world (Anthony Masters)

Young Hippo
Young Hippo adventure
Young Hippo animal
Young Hippo funny
Young Hippo magic
Young Hippo school
Young Hippo spooky
Young Hippo sport
Young Puffin
Young Puffin modern classics
Young Puffin storybooks

ZPTV

Young adult series

@café (US)

Adlib

Bantam action
Bondi Place (Jason Herbison)
Boyfriend Club (Janet Quin-Harkin)
Bright sparks
Bug files (US)

City Hospital (Keith Miles)
Confessions
Contents
Clueless

Dark enchantment
Discworld (Terry Pratchett)
Doctor Who
Double Click Cafe

Emergency (Lisa Rojany) (US)
Extreme zone (M C Sumner)

Fear Street (R L Stine)
Fighting fantasy

Highflyers (Judy Allen)
Hodder fantasy
Hodder supernatural
Hodder SF
Hodder thrillers
Hollyoaks
Horrorscopes

J-17 love

Karen Cady mysteries (Penny Kline)

Lone Wolf
Love stories

Making friends (Kate Andrews)
Making out (Katherine Applegate)
Making waves (Katherine Applegate)
Models (Chloe Rayban)
Models move on (Chloe Rayban)

Night world (L J Smith)

Nightmares

Ocean City (Katherine Applegate)
Orchard black apple

Point
Point crime
Point fantasy
Point horror
Point horror unleashed
Point nurses
Point romance
Point romance: forget me not
Point SF
Psychic zone (Mathew Stone)

Redwall (Brian Jacques)

Sabrina the teenage witch
Saved by the Bell
Signature
St Jo's hospital (Sue Welford)
Star Trek
Star Wars
Surfside High
Sunset Island
Suspense
Sweet dreams
Sweet Valley High (Kate William)
Sweet Valley University (Laurie John)

Tear jerkers
Terror Academy (US)
The Bill

X-Files
Xtreme

Zodiac chillers

Series

Current children's book prizes for fiction

This information supplied by Young Book Trust

Angus Book Award

An Angus-wide initiative to encourage pupils to read quality teenage fiction. From January to March, third year pupils read the five shortlisted titles, chosen by teachers and librarians from books published in paperback in the preceding 12 months and written by an author resident in the UK. The books are discussed before the children vote in a secret ballot. For further details contact Moyra Hood, Education Resource Librarian, Angus Council, tel: 01242 435008.

1996	*Night after tomorrow*	Sue Welford	Oxford University Press
1997	*Tunnel vision*	Malcolm Rose	Scholastic Press
1998	*Unbeliever*	Robert Swindells	Puffin

Birmingham Cable Children's Book Awards
(previously known as the TSB Birmingham Children's Book Awards)

These awards, administered by the Birmingham Readers & Writers' Festival in association with Birmingham Education Department, exist to encourage the children of Birmingham to take an active interest in current fiction. Judging is in three stages. In the first stage children from four Birmingham schools, two from each age group - 7 to 11 years and 12 to 16 years - select a shortlist of ten books (five from each age group). In the second stage children from 12 schools read and discuss each of the shortlisted books. In the third stage, two children from each school meet to select a winning book for each age group. Books submitted must be works of fiction by British authors published in the UK for the first time in the previous year (e.g. 1997 for the 1998 award). Further details from Matthew Gidley, tel: 0121 303 4244 fax: 0121 233 9702 email: readers.writers@dial.pipex.com.

1996	7-11	*Little Wolf's book of badness*	Ian Whybrow	Hodder
	12-16	*Bokkie*	Toeckey Jones	Bodley Head
1997	7-11	*Goosebumps: Wailing special*	R L Stine	Scholastic Press
	12-16	*The final journey*	Gudrun Pausewang	Penguin
1998		*Harry Potter and the philosopher's stone*	J K Rowling	Bloomsbury

The Caldecott Medal

This award is presented for the most distinguished American picture book for children published during the preceding year. It was named after the English illustrator Randolph Caldecott (1846-86). Instituted in 1938.

1994	Grandfather's journey	Allen Say	Houghton
1995	Smoky night	Eve Bunting Illus. David Diaz	Harcourt Brace Jovanovich
1996	Officer Buckle and Gloria	Peggy Rathman	Putnam
1997	Golem	David Wisniewski	Clarion Books
1998	Rapunzel	Paul O Zelinsky	Dutton Children's Books
1999	Snowflake Bentley	Jacqueline Briggs Martin Illus. Mary Azarian	Houghton

Carnegie and Greenaway Award

The Carnegie and the Kate Greenaway awards are presented annually by the Library Association and administered by the Youth Libraries Group of the Library Association. Nominations are submitted by Library Association members. The selection panel consists of 13 children's librarians.

The Carnegie Medal

The Carnegie medal is given for an outstanding work of fiction or non-fiction for children. Contenders are appraised for characterisation, plot, style, accuracy, imaginative quality and that indefinable element that lifts a book above the others. (NB The date of this award is based on the year in which the books were published, not in which the award is announced, e.g. the 1993 award was announced in June 1994). Instituted in 1936.

1993	Stone cold	Robert Swindells	Hamish Hamilton
1994	Whispers in the graveyard	Theresa Breslin	Methuen
1995	His dark materials: Northern lights	Philip Pullman	Scholastic
1996	Junk	Melvin Burgess	Andersen Press
1997	River boy	Tim Bowler	Oxford University Press

The Kate Greenaway Medal

The Kate Greenaway Medal goes to an artist who has produced the most distinguished work in the illustration of children's books. The nominated books are assessed for design, format and production as well as artistic merit. The books must be published in the United Kingdom during the preceding year. Instituted in 1955.

1993	Black ships before Troy	Alan Lee	Frances Lincoln
1994	Way home	Gregory Rogers	Andersen Press
1995	The Christmas miracle of Jonathan Toomey	P J Lynch	Walker Books
1996	The baby who wouldn't go to bed	Helen Cooper	Doubleday
1997	When Jessie came across the sea	Amy Hest Illus. P J Lynch	Walker Books

Prizes

The Children's Book Award is organised by the Federation of Children's Book Groups and is supported by The Paul Hamlyn Foundation. The award, made annually since 1980, is for the best book of the year, judged by the children themselves. Thousands of children from all over the country help the Federation to test the books. The author of the award-winning book receives a glass bowl, specially commissioned from a leading British craftworker and engraved with a theme from the book, together with a portfolio compiled from comments, letters and drawings from the children taking part in the testing. The information about the year's books which is collected during the testing, is compiled into a 'pick of the year' booklist of tried and tested books.

1994	Overall and Longer Novel Winner		
	The boy in the bubble	Ian Strachan	Methuen
	Picture Book Winner		
	Amazing Anthony Ant	Lorna and Graham Philpot	Orion
	Shorter Novel Winner		
	The finders	Nigel Hinton	Viking
1995	Overall and Shorter Novel Winner		
	Harriet's hare	Dick King-Smith	Doubleday
	Picture Book Winner		
	The rascally cake	Jeanne Willis Illus: Korky Paul	Andersen Press
	Longer Novel Winner		
	Walk two moons	Sharon Creech	PanMacmillan
1996	Overall and Longer Novel Winner		
	Double act	Jacqueline Wilson	Doubleday
	Picture Book Winner		
	Solo	Paul Geraghty	Hutchinson
	Shorter Novel Winner		
	The wreck of the Zanzibar	Michael Morpurgo	Heinemann
1997	Overall and Shorter Novel Winner		
	The hundred-mile-an-hour dog	Jeremy Strong	Viking
	Picture Book Winner		
	Mr Bear to the rescue	Debi Gliori	Orchard Books
	Longer Novel Winner		
	Which way is home?	Ian Strachan	Mammoth
1998	Overall and Longer Novel Winner		
	Harry Potter and the philosopher's stone	J K Rowling	Bloomsbury
	Picture Book Winner		
	The lion who wanted to love	Giles Andreae	Orchard Books
	Shorter Novel Winner		
	Nightmare stairs	Robert Swindells	Doubleday

Prizes

The biennial Children's Laureate will be awarded to an eminent British writer or illustrator of children's books both to celebrate a lifetime's achievement and to spotlight the role of children's book creators in making the readers of the future. This working prize will provide a platform for the winner to stimulate public discussion about the importance of children's literature and reading in a forward-looking society. Administered by the British section of IBBY (International Board on Books for Young People).

The Fidler Award
(originally known as the Kathleen Fidler Award)

This award was set up in 1980 to encourage new authors to submit their work for the 8 to 12 age group. It is sponsored by Hodder Children's Books who undertake publication of the winning manuscript, and administered by Scottish Book Trust. The winner is then published by Blackie. The prize is £1,000 plus a trophy. Further information is available from Scottish Book Trust, tel: 0131 229 3663.

1993	*48 hours with Franklin*	Mij Kelly	Blackie
1994	*Run, Zan, run*	Catherine MacPhail	Blackie
1995	*Edge of danger*	Clare Dudman	Dutton
1996	*The falcon's quest*	John Smirthwaite	Hodder
1997	*Slate mountain*	Mark Leyland	Hodder
1998	Not awarded		

Guardian Children's Fiction Award

Prizes

The Guardian Children's Fiction Award has been given annually since 1967 for an outstanding work of fiction for children by a British or Commonwealth author, which was first published in the United Kingdom during the preceding year. The award is chosen by a panel of authors and *The Guardian* children's books review editor. Picture books are not included.

1994	*The Mennyms*	Sylvia Waugh	Julia MacRae
1995	*Maphead*	Lesley Howarth	Walker Books
1996	Joint Winners		
	His dark materials: Northern lights	Philip Pullman	Scholastic Press
	The Sherwood hero	Alison Prince	Macmillan Children's Books
1997	*Junk*	Melvin Burgess	Andersen Press
1998	*Fire, bed and bone*	Henrietta Branford	Walker Books

IBBY Honour List

The IBBY (International Board on Books for Young People) Honour List is a biennial selection of outstanding recently published books, honouring writers, illustrators and translators from IBBY member countries. The titles, selected by the National Sections, must represent the best in children's literature from each country and be suitable for publication throughout the world, thus furthering the IBBY objective of encouraging international understanding through children's literature. The books are shown in five parallel travelling exhibitions before they are kept as permanent deposits in some of the world's leading children's book institutions. The following are the British Section nominations for the 1998 IBBY Honour List:

Author nomination	*The wreck of the Zanzibar*	Michael Morpurgo	Mammoth
Illustration nomination	*Clown*	Quentin Blake	Jonathan Cape
Translator nomination	*No roof in Bosnia*	Patrician Crampton	Spindlewood

The Kurt Maschler Award — Announced in November/December

The Kurt Maschler Award was established in 1982 by the late Kurt Maschler for a work of imagination for children, in which text and illustration are excellent and presented so that each enhances, yet balances, the other. The prize is £1,000 and in addition the winner receives an 'Emil', a bronze figure of Erich Kastner's famous character, cast by Diana Welch. It was Kurt Maschler's publishing company, William Verlag, which originally published *Emil and the Detectives*. The judges are leading experts in children's literature.

1993	*Think of an eel*	Karen Wallace	Walker Books
1994	*So much*	Trish Cook and Helen Oxenbury	Walker Books
1995	*The little boat*	Kathy Henderson and Patrick Benson	Walker Books
1996	*Drop dead*	Babette Cole	Jonathan Cape
1997	*Lady Muck*	William Mayne Illus. Jonathan Heale	Heinemann
1998	*Voices in the park*	Anthony Browne	Doubleday

Prizes

Lancashire County Library Children's Books of the Year Award Announced in June

This award is for a work of fiction suitable for the 11 to 14 age group, published in the UK between 1 September and 31 August of the previous year. It is sponsored by National Westminster Bank and organised by Lancashire County Library. The judging panel consists of 11 to 14 year old pupils from secondary schools in Lancashire. Further details, and copies of the reviews of shortlisted books written by the judges, from David Lightfoot, Lancashire County Library HQ, 143 Corporation Street, Preston PR1 2UQ.

1996	Chandra	Frances Mary Hendry	Oxford University Press
1997	Sea of peril	Elizabeth Hawkins	Orchard Books
1998	Jay	Elizabeth Laird	Mammoth

NASEN Special Educational Needs Award Announced in November

The NASEN Award is organised by the National Association for Special Educational Needs and the Educational Publishers Council. The prize is awarded for a book which enhances the knowledge and understanding of those engaged in the education of children with special needs. A children's award was given for the first time in 1994 for a book written for children under 16, which does most to put forward a positive image of children with special educational needs.

1996	How to write really badly	Anne Fine	Metheun
1997	Charlie's eye	Dorothy Horgan	Hamish Hamilton
1998	The crowstarver	Dick King-Smith	Doubleday

The Newbery Medal Announced in January/February

This is the most important American award, given annually for the most distinguished contribution to American literature for children. It is conferred upon books published during the previous year. The award is named after John Newbery (1713-1767), a London bookseller and first British publisher of children's books. Instituted in 1922. The recipient must be a citizen or resident of the United States.

1994	The giver	Lois Lowry	Houghton
1995	Walk two moons	Sharon Creech	Harper Collins
1996	The midwife apprentice	Karen Cushman	Clarion Books
1997	The view from Saturday	E L Konigsburg	Atheneum
1998	Out of the dust	Karen Hesse	Scholastic Press
1999	Holes	Louis Sachar	Farrar Straus & Giroux

Prizes

Set up in 1989, the Sheffield Children's Book Award is presented annually to the book chosen by the children of Sheffield as the most enjoyable. The majority of the judges look at, read and vote on the shortlisted books within their class at school. Additional copies of all the books are available through local libraries and at W Hartley Seed's West Street Bookshop where interested people can register their vote. *The Sheffield Telegraph* prints short reviews of all the books in a double-page spread, which also includes a voting slip. The Award began in 1989. There are three category winners. For further information contact Jennifer Wilson, tel: 0114 250 6840.

1993	0-6 Category winner		
	I won't bite	Rod Campbell	Campbell Books
	7-11 Category and overall winner		
	The dog that dug	Jonathan Long Illus. Korky Paul	Bodley Head
	12+ Category winner		
	Gulf	Robert Westall	Methuen
1994	0-6 Category winner		
	The Queen's knickers	Nicholas Allan	Hutchinson
	7-11 Category and overall winner		
	Haddock 'n' chips	Linda Hoy Illus. Caroline Holden	Walker Books
	12+ Category winner		
	Stone cold	Robert Swindells	Hamish Hamilton
1995	0-6 Category winner		
	Isobel's noisy tummy	David McKee	Andersen Press
	7-11 Category and overall winner		
	Beware the killer coat	Susan Gates	Walker Books
	12+ Category winner		
	A time of fire	Robert Westall	Macmillan
1996	0-6 Category winner		
	The last noo noo	Jill Murphy	Walker Books
	7-11 Category and overall winner		
	Double act	Jacqueline Wilson Illus. Nick Sharratt & Sue Heap	Doubleday
	12+ Category winner		
	Unbeliever	Robert Swindells	Hamish Hamilton
1997	0-6 Category and overall winner		
	A cheese and tomato spider	Nick Sharratt	Scholastic Press
	7-11 Category winner		
	Bad girls	Jacqueline Wilson	Transworld
	12+ Category winner		
	Death or glory boys	Theresa Breslin	Reed
1998	0-6 Category winner		
	Mucky pup	Ken Brown	Andersen Press
	7-11 Category winner		
	Pirate pandemonium	Jeremy Strong	A & C Black
	12+ Category and overall winner		
	Harry Potter and the philosopher's stone	J K Rowling	Bloomsbury

Prizes

The Smarties Book Prize was established to encourage high standards and stimulate interest in books for children. It is sponsored by Smarties and administrated by Book Trust. Eligible books are those published during the preceding year, written in English by a citizen of the UK, or an author resident in the UK. The author must be living at the time of publication. Gold, Silver and Bronze Awards are given in each of three age categories, 5 and under, 6 to 8 years and 9 to 11 years. Winners of the Gold Award receive £2,500; Silver, £1,500; Bronze, £500. Since 1996 the winners have been selected by young judges from a shortlist drawn up by adult judges. Posters and bookmarks, as well as details of how to be a young judge, are available from Book Trust, tel: 0181 870 9055.

1994	0-5 Category winner		
	So much	Trish Cooke Illus. Helen Oxenbury	Walker Books
	6-8 Category winner		
	Dimanche Diller	Henrietta Branford Illus. Lesley Harker	Young Lions
	Overall and 9-11 Category winner		
	The exiles at home	Hilary McKay	Gollancz
1995	0-5 Category winner		
	The last noo noo	Jill Murphy	Walker Books
	6-8 Category winner		
	Thomas and the tinners	Jill Paton Walsh	Macdonald Young Books
	Overall and 9-11 Category winner		
	Double act	Jacqueline Wilson	Doubleday
	Joint 9-11 Category winner		
	Weather eye	Elizabeth Howarth	Walker Books
1996	Gold Award Winners		
Under 5	*Oops!*	Colin McNaughton	Andersen Press
6-8	*The butterfly lion*	Michael Morpurgo	Collins Children's Books
9-11	*The firework-maker's daughter*	Philip Pullman	Yearling
1997	Gold Award Winners		
Under 5	*Leon and Bob*	Simon James	Walker Books
6-8	*The owl tree*	Jenny Nimmo	Walker Books
9-11	*Harry Potter and the philosopher's stone*	J K Rowling	Bloomsbury
1998	Gold Award Winners		
Under 5	*Cowboy baby*	Sue Heap	Walker Books
6-8	*The last gold diggers*	Harry Horse	Puffin Books
9-11	*Harry Potter and the chamber of secrets*	J K Rowling	Bloomsbury

Prizes

Children from 60 Stockport schools are asked to select their favourite books. The aim of the project is to raise the profile of reading for pleasure, offer children the best new fiction and create a community of readers in school. For further information contact: Andrea Ellison, Head of Library Services to Children, The Dialstone Centre, Lisburne Lane, Stockport, SK2 7L tel: 0161 474 2250/2251 fax: 0161 483 0950 email: sls@rmplc.co.uk.

1998

Key Stage 1 winner	*Thud*	Nick Butterworth	Collins
Key Stage 2 winner	*The Lottie project*	Jacqueline Wilson	Doubleday
Key Stage 3 winner	*Nightmare stairs*	Robert Swindells	Doubleday
Key Stage 4 winner	*Iron heads*	Susan Gates	Oxford University Press

The Whitbread Children's Book of the Year was first awarded in 1972. The award goes to a book for children aged seven years and up, published in the UK or Republic of Ireland, written by a British or Irish author or one who is living in Britain or Ireland. It is sponsored by Whitbread and administered by the Booksellers Association. The award is worth £8,000.

1994	*Gold dust*	Geraldine McCaughrean	Oxford University Press
1995	*The wreck of the Zanzibar*	Michael Morpurgo	Methuen
1996	*The Tulip touch*	Anne Fine	Hamish Hamilton
1997	*Aquila*	Andrew Norris	Hamish Hamilton
1998	*Skellig*	David Almond	Hodder

Prizes

Bibliography

There are many specialist reference books and periodicals which provide information on children's authors. The following list highlights some that you may find especially useful. They should be available through your local library.

Books

- *Children's fiction index* 7th Ed 1993
  Edited by Jennifer Madden and Margaret Hobson
  ISBN 0 900092 85 8
  Association of Assistant Librarians

- *Children's sequels* 9th Ed 1999
  Edited by Margaret Hobson
  Library Association

- *Oxford companion to children's literature* 1999
  Edited by Humphrey Carpenter and Mari Prichard
  ISBN 0 19 860228 6
  Oxford University Press

- *Twentieth-century children's writers* 3rd Ed 1989
  ISBN 0 912289 95 3
  St James Press (USA)

- *100 best books: Books for up to 16 year olds* 1998
  Published each year
  Young Book Trust

- *A multicultural guide to children's books for up to 12s* 1994
  Compiled by Judith Elkin with Steve Rosson
  Edited by Rosemary Stones
  Books for Keeps

Periodicals

- *Books for keeps: The children's book magazine*
  Books for Keeps
  6 Brightfield Read
  London SE12 8QF
  Six issues per year

- *Carousel: The guide to children's books*
  Carousel
  7 Carrs Lane
  Birmingham B4 7TG
  Three issues per year

- *The school librarian*
  Four issues per year
  School Library Association

CD-ROM

- *Book wizard* is now available in some public and school libraries

Index

Index

Author	Age ranges	Page numbers

Index

Author	Age ranges	Page numbers

Index

Index

Index

Norah Irvin and Lesley Cooper are qualified librarians, with many years' experience of working with children and young people, in schools and in the public libraries of Hertfordshire.

Their careers with Hertfordshire Library Service and Hertfordshire Schools Library Service have provided them with the opportunity to:

- formulate book selection policy for the county
- advise schools on library and book provision
- advise parent/teacher groups on reading
- select stock for schools and Schools Library Service centres
- run courses for teachers on using books with children
- give book talks in both schools and public libraries

When working as Promotion and Marketing Co-ordinator for Hertfordshire Library Service, Norah was responsible for the development in Hertfordshire of *Bookstart*. Designed 'to bring books to babies' through health centres, the project also included a video to alert parents to the importance of using books with very young children.

Having been an advisor in schools library centres, Lesley is presently the Librarian in a local boys school, and continues to work with Hertfordshire Schools Library Service.